MW00587743

FRAME WORK

GLUCKMAN MAYNER ARCHITECTS
ESSAY BY DETLEF MERTINS

FRAME
WORK

NANCY —

TO A GREAT ARCHITECTURAL PATRON
THANKS FOR EVERYTHING, WE LOVE
WORKING WITH YOU

THE MONACELLI PRESS

Library of Congress Cataloging-in-Publication Data
Gluckman Mayner Architects.
Framework : Gluckman Mayner Architects / essay by Detlef Mertins. — 1st ed.
p.   cm.
ISBN 978-1-58093-225-7
1. Gluckman Mayner Architects. 2. Architecture, Modern—20th century.
3. Architecture, Modern—21st century. I. Mertins, Detlef. II. Title. III.
Title: Gluckman Mayner Architects.
NA737.G545G68   2009
720.92'2—dc22   2009005960

Printed in China

www.monacellipress.com

10 9 8 7 6 5 4 3 2 1
First edition

Project Editor: Scott Watson
Design by Omnivore

CONTENTS

Architecture is a collaborative profession.

This collaboration begins in the studio with discussion and speculation among the design team. Our work environment encourages interaction and investigation. We utilize sketches, virtual computer studies, and three-dimensional models to advance our initial concepts.

Engineers and consultants join the team at an early stage in a fully integrated approach to design. The delineation of the building's structural expression and the organization of other building systems become fundamental aspects of the design: physical frame influences form.

Our clients are equally part of the collaboration, and we particularly value those individuals and institutions who work with us to articulate a clear program, explore context, remain open to risks, and above all, engage in an ongoing exchange that might culminate in an unexpected (and often improved) result.

This approach to architecture was forged by my experiences working with site-specific artists in the late 1970s—work that continues to this day. Artists such as Dan Flavin, Jenny Holzer, and Richard Serra employed architectural means to establish a new and immediate relationship between the viewer, the object, and the space they occupy. I am convinced that the opportunity for a significant architecture exists in the resonance generated by the art and the space it inhabits.

The work produced in our studio respects this dynamic. We imagine how space will be occupied by its users, realizing that the relationship of the viewer to the space is fundamental to the success of the project.

Our architecture, by its very nature, is inclusive. Our buildings are characterized by clarity: clarity of form, clarity of structure, clarity of spatial diagram, clarity of materiality and detail.

To me, architecture is the subjective application of objective criteria. Nevertheless, it's not architecture until it's built. Thanks to all of the collaborators, co-conspirators, colleagues, contractors, and clients—everyone who has participated in this challenging, rewarding, and mysterious process. —RG

DETLEF MERTINS

THE MOMENT OF IMMEDIACY

As criticisms of late modernism destabilized architectural culture in the 1970s, many architects looked to historical styles and populist imagery to invest their work with meaning. Richard Gluckman, on the other hand, discovered that meaning itself could be redefined within modernism by learning from a certain species of minimalist art.[1] Through his early involvement with the Dia Foundation and artists such as Walter De Maria, Dan Flavin, Donald Judd, and Richard Serra, he developed an approach to design that remained distinctive even as more and more architects were touched by the ascetic imperative. While minimalism in architecture has generally assumed the guise of a more extreme version of modernist form—more tautly abstract and crystalline, more ruthless in its suppression of windows, doors, moldings, and flashings, often coupled with a richer palette of materials or luminous lighting—Gluckman went further from the start, learning other, more structural lessons as well. He recognized that the role of architecture changed when, in the 1960s, artists sought to engage it more actively by pulling their work off the wall and into the space of the viewer—into the real spaces of galleries, warehouses, city streets, and landscapes—reframing architecture as it was framed by it. Gluckman absorbed this turn so thoroughly that he was soon able to adapt the strategies developed for displaying art to mediate other kinds of experiences as well.

Gluckman's exposure to artists who broke with modernist abstraction came in 1977 when Heiner Friedrich and Philippa de Menil commissioned a renovation of their Manhattan town house, including the installation of works by Cy Twombly and Blinky Palermo as well as by De Maria, Judd, and Flavin. Flavin's work was especially eye-opening for substituting fluorescent lamps for architectural moldings and transforming spaces such as stairs into volumes of colored light. It was Flavin, Gluckman recalls, who first eliminated baseboards, transforming walls and floors into pure planes against which to situate his work. A few years later, the architect participated in the installation of De Maria's **Broken Kilometer** in a Soho loft, a work and a setting that broke decisively from the immersive environment of white cube galleries, which had become popular for displaying abstract art.[2] By isolating art

from the outside world, eliminating windows, and neutralizing architectural features, these galleries had suspended both art and viewer in a timeless and transcendent world. Reduced to pure perception, stripped of worldliness, and disembodied, the viewer, in this mode of reception, dissolved through immersion in the art object. This mystification of the artwork was soon criticized for its claims to authority, power, and value. In contrast, De Maria used the old pressed-metal ceiling, cast-iron columns with classical capitals, and sprinkler pipes of the existing building as foil for his piece. At the same time, its rows of brass rods, arranged with machine precision on the old hardwood floor, served to recalibrate the rhythm of the space. The reciprocal inflections between the art and the architecture implied a definition of abstraction situated in the world itself, not outside or above it. Here abstraction was revealed as a procedure, rather than a thing, a procedure for measuring the world and negotiating the relationship between geometry and matter, embodiment and disembodiment; it no longer represented one side of such binary oppositions. Gluckman recognized that by using architectural means, artists such as Flavin and De Maria were able to achieve a "new and immediate relationship between the viewer, the object, and the space around it."[3] Placed in an unexpected and more awkward perspective, the viewer was launched into a space of action, having to grapple with the work in its difference and from a stance that remained unstable and contingent. Gluckman's work as an architect has consistently explored the potential of such three-way relationships to generate a sense of immediacy in time and place and, through it, a heightened awareness of self in a field of relationships at once social and corporeal. Where the white cube galleries had constructed the viewing of art as if it were unmediated, Gluckman used rudimentary architectural elements—columns, trusses, walls, floors, ceilings, skylights, doorways, windows, lighting, and color—to stage that experience as an experience.

In his renovations for the Dia Center for the Arts in New York (1987), the Andy Warhol Museum in Pittsburgh (1994), and the many galleries and museums featured in this book, Gluckman heeded Flavin's example as well as Friedrich's explicit directive to put aside the typical modality of design in order to see the spaces of existing buildings for what they were. He developed techniques of editing—removing, resurfacing, painting, lighting—that were modest yet strategic for clarifying their architectonic logic and bringing their character into sharper relief. The difference between this approach and the imposition of a totalizing new order and language cannot be overemphasized. Without such restraint, it would be impossible to achieve the effect that Hal Foster observed in writing of the Dia Center: "The spaces work both ways: they can frame the art when required (as in the beautiful Robert Ryman exhibition of 1988–89), or be framed by the art when it projects a space of its own (as in the luminous Robert Irwin installation of 1998)."[4] Making a building more legible as itself reiterated the modernist ethos of self-reflexive self-definition, while treating it as the background to an event rather than the event itself. Doing this with historic buildings—even warehouses and industrial buildings similar to those that had inspired early modernists—no longer produced pure and timeless forms but rather intensified the historicity of these buildings as well as the immediacy of the present.

In designing commercial galleries, Gluckman discovered that it was not necessary to abandon the paradigm of the white cube. It took only a few architectural elements or spatial qualities to quietly break the transcendental spell while still supporting intense and focused artistic experience. Consider, for instance, the exposed roof construction at the Mary Boone Gallery in New York (2000). The experience of a painting in this space is altered by the rough wooden trusses arcing to meet the wall; freed from the rest of the roof, they become figures in space that cross the zone of the skylight. Carefully tempering expression with restraint, the trusses attract attention without overwhelming the art; they invite the eye to shift back and forth between painting and ceiling, and perhaps even to wander out the door, pausing momentarily to take in a small painting at the side.

Or consider the role played by the deep wells of the skylights at the Gagosian Gallery Twenty-first Street, in the same Chelsea neighborhood (2006). The space involves what Gluckman calls a scale shift: it is grander and more monumental in scale than the spaces we ordinarily inhabit, making us aware of our bodies and **their** scale while animating our relationship to the space. The yellow bricks on the outside are larger than ordinary bricks, the doors taller than ordinary doors, raising expectations that something exceptional will occur inside. There are no extraneous features or details to distract, no lighting track (just individual halogen lights) or ventilation grills (just narrow slots along the ceiling edge). The only things visible are abstract surfaces so recessive that they effectively disappear. Yet the depth, width, and length of the skylights give them a monumental presence—even as voids—and bring them into silent dialogue with the art and the viewer. They charge the room and give it a direction counter to the axis of entry,

promoting a greater awareness of being in the space with the work and of the work being in the space with us. Such elements have no meaning in themselves, no semiotic coding to transmit; rather they serve to destabilize expectations, inhibit absorption in the work, and heighten the sense of encounter. Meaning is treated here not as something given in advance but as something constructed in situ and in play; it becomes an effect of the experiences induced by the art, which may then be remembered and narrated.

Gluckman's first opportunity to rework his techniques for other uses came with fashion stores for Helmut Lang and Gianni Versace (1997), where display was still the key function and relation to the body remained a key issue. Inspired by Tony Smith's work, he used oversized rectangular boxes to mediate between the scale of the body and the volume of the space, effecting the sense of immediacy and surprise produced in his galleries. Gluckman capitalizes on the fact that display is often a part of other programs or latent in them—in museums, stores, and libraries, even churches, spas, houses, and apartments. By reducing elements such as shelving, tables, bathtubs, and kitchen counters to sharply delineated geometric forms, altering their scale or the viewer's perspective, he effectively frames and elevates the everyday activities they support. Shopping, dining, bathing, and cooking are put on display and brought into sharper focus.

Like Serra, Gluckman often begins with simple geometries, manipulating them to produce complex effects through combination, rotation, and inflection. The entry pavilion of the Mori Arts Center in Tokyo (2003) wraps a delicate glass screen around five levels of circulation hung from a funnel-shaped concrete core. Its bowing bell shape is a cable-net structure created with elliptical hoops, undulating in width, that support the glass—like a hoop skirt. The furling facade of brick and glass at One Kenmare Square in New York (2006) was constructed, both geometrically and physically, one floor at a time. Each layer is a sine wave identical to the one below, but slipped sideways and stepped back to create the impression of a moving surface. The repetition of a single continuous wave made it possible to use the same formwork on all levels. Most recently, the Perelman Building at the Philadelphia Museum of Art (2007) features a warped wall along the galleria that links the addition to the historic building. By offsetting the corbelled wall of rough-faced cast stone by six feet at the bottom of one end, Gluckman made the geometry of the space trapezoidal, facilitating movement, diffusing sunlight, and heightening the transition from light areas to dark. Such geometric and material manipulations create formal ambiguities that intrigue observers and encourage them to explore themselves observing and become aware of the vagaries and strange pleasures of vision in motion.

Other projects have exploited the plasticity of vision through the active movement of the viewer or inhabitant.

At the Gagosian Gallery Twenty-fourth Street in New York (2000), the awareness and mutability of scale is intensified as we move from one gallery to the next—each different in size and proportion but not height. On a highly constrained site in the Bronx, the Iglesia Evangelica de Co-Op City (2005) is organized around processional movement that heightens the participatory experience of gathering together for services and special events such as weddings, funerals, and confirmations. Similarly, it is movement that brings the Matchbox House on Long Island (2001) to life, turning its compact configuration of spaces into a dynamic device for activating the experience of the landscape and taking its measure. Like a movie camera, the house channels and links views while also unfolding expansive panoramas.

Moving elements—large doors and sliding walls—likewise play an important role as mediators in Gluckman's projects, enabling occupants to alter spatial and social relationships at will. In the original Gagosian Gallery in Soho (1991), the overhead door of the former garage was simply exchanged for one with frosted glass, allowing the gallery to open dramatically to the street—letting the space of the street and the space of the gallery flow into one another through a frame so large that it almost disappears from view. Replacing the opaque panels in the garage door with frosted glass, Gluckman turned it into a sign of openness even when the gallery was closed, while also creating a sense of mystery and expectation. More recently, he equipped the four main galleries of the Mori Arts Center with movable walls that let curators modulate the degree of openness or closure, orchestrate the sequence from one to the next, and control the relationship to the surrounding observation deck. At a domestic scale, the Tribeca Loft in New York (2003) provides an even greater range of modulation with walls of canvas and translucent plastic that can reconfigure the space for the couple, a dinner party for twelve, a cocktail party for fifty, or an overnight guest. Gluckman's favorite arrangement is one that surprised him: the clients isolated a portion of the space to be entirely inaccessible.

Be they for art or everyday life, Gluckman's buildings effectively elide the opposition between absorption and theatricality, which the critic Michael Fried had made central to the interpretation of modern art. They also sidestep a similar opposition between tectonics and spectacle proffered in architecture by Kenneth Frampton in the 1980s. Rather, Gluckman's work eschews such either/or categorizations. It is absorbing and theatrical, abstract and relational, material and mise-en-scène. This species of modernism is not fixated on a fundamentalism of pure form or a morality of honest construction. Like the ancient ascetic impulse that has operated across cultures and times, it mediates such oppositions on an active basis.[5] This kind of reductivism—using geometry to discipline matter and construction to materialize geometry—produces results that bracket the existence of worldly objects

and the subjective acts through which they are made to appear. It recalls less the Christian version of asceticism, with its emphasis on transcending self, and more the pre-Christian, which focused on self-mastery as a form of control originally available to only a few through extensive learning, discipline, and culture, yet public and civic in orientation. From whitewashing found spaces to suspending glass cubes in the air or giving torque to masonry walls, Gluckman's mastery of the formal and material practices of architecture leads not out of struggle or uncertainty but into it and into the always surprising moment of immediacy.

NOTES
1. For a summary of the issues associated with minimalist art, including the distinction between two kinds of minimalism, see Rosalind Krauss, "Overcoming the Limits of Matter: On Revising Minimalism," in American Art of the 1960s 1 (New York: Museum of Modern Art, 1991): 123–41.
2. See Brian O'Doherty, Inside the White Cube: The Ideology of the Gallery Space (San Francisco: Lapis Press, 1976).
3. Richard Gluckman, in Space Framed: Richard Gluckman Architect (New York: The Monacelli Press, 2000), 180.
4. Hal Foster, "Illuminated Structure, Embodied Space," in Space Framed, 184.
5. For a treatment of asceticism both inside and outside Christian transcendentalism, see Geoffrey Galt Harpham, The Ascetic Imperative in Culture and Criticism (Chicago: University of Chicago Press, 1987).

GAGOSIAN GALLERY
TWENTY-FOURTH STREET
NEW YORK, NEW YORK
2000

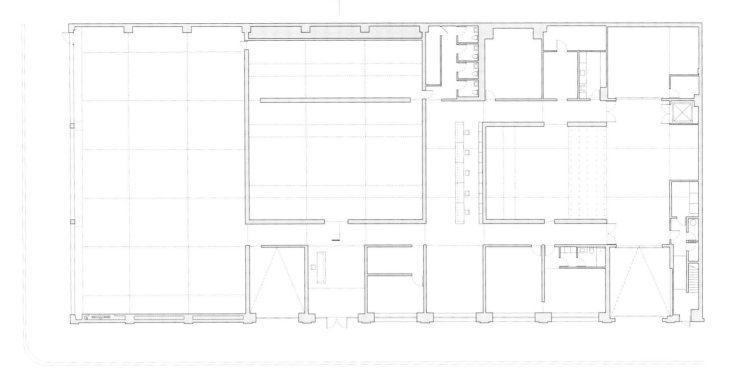

This 26,000-square-foot gallery has the scale of a small museum. The 100-foot-long roof trusses of the former trucking distribution facility have been raised ten feet to accommodate large-scale art work. Inserted into the newly created space is a plastic clerestory that disperses light throughout the venue and establishes a prominent "sign" visible from the West Side Highway. The facades are unified by enlarging some window openings to incorporate aluminum and glass panels and infilling others with masonry. Exhibition spaces include a main gallery with 60-foot-long ribbon skylights, two smaller sky-lit galleries, special purpose gallery, small prints and video showroom, and private showroom with 23-foot-high display walls. The simple tectonics of the plastic, gypsum board, and concrete contrast with the resawn pine used for the furnishings.

Richard Gluckman (principal); Michael Hamilton (project architect); Elena Cannon, Wilmay Choy, Ching-Loong Tai, Celia Chiang, David Pysh (design team)

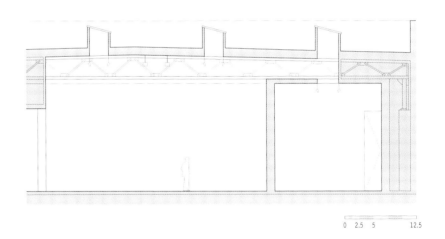

MARY BOONE GALLERY
CHELSEA
NEW YORK, NEW YORK
2000

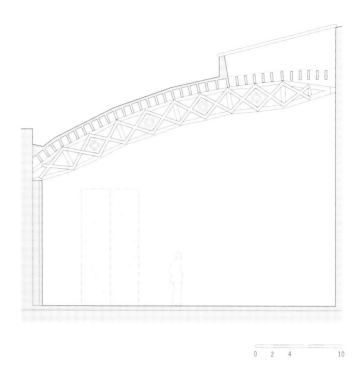

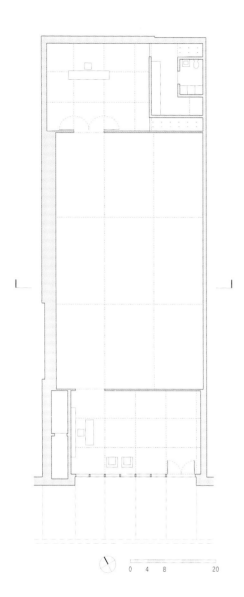

This Chelsea gallery complements the client's uptown exhibition space, which was designed by Gluckman Mayner Architects in 1995. New, highly refined finishes contrast with the original crude wood trusses. A center wall obviated the need for the original tie bars; the space now accommodates a major painting wall. Lighting this wall from the top emphasizes the altered spatial hierarchy of the building. Natural light is introduced into each of the other spaces: a small central skylight illuminates the back room, while a floor-to-ceiling translucent-glass storefront enlivens the reception area. These ancillary areas feature 13-foot-high tinted plaster ceilings that accentuate the volume and materiality of the main space. The limited palette of materials includes a steel-troweled concrete floor, aluminum plate shelves, and aluminum laminate storage units.

Richard Gluckman (principal); Michael Hamilton (project architect); Daniel Gallagher, William Truitt (design team)

AUSTIN MUSEUM OF ART
AUSTIN, TEXAS
2001

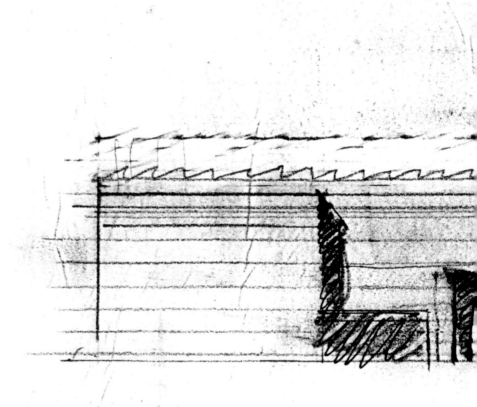

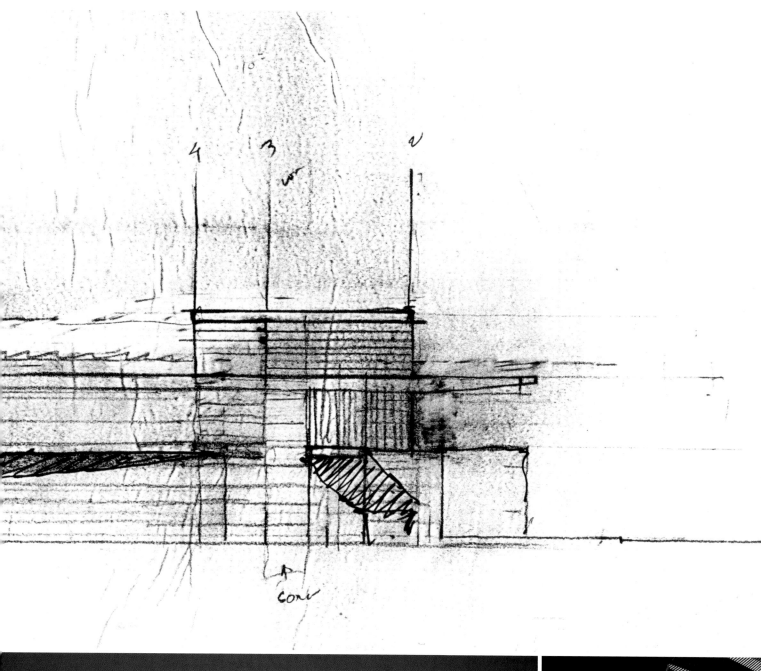

Planned for the southern edge of Republic Park in the center of downtown Austin, this proposal for a 148,000-square-foot museum seeks to provide a clarity of form and experience. The building contains an array of galleries organized around a circulation path that relies on the lobby and interior courts to maintain the visitor's orientation. The spaces include two "centerpiece" galleries for major traveling exhibitions, large gallery for contemporary art, art and technology gallery, sculpture garden, and five galleries for the permanent collection. Also included in the museum are an education center with multipurpose classrooms, children's hands-on gallery and orientation center, 300-seat theater, restaurant, and store. Tempered natural light enriches the gallery and public areas within the museum. Translucent glass walls in the art and technology gallery above the lobby serve as a projection surface and allow for public presentation of art at an urban scale. Set back on the site, the museum links its entrance plaza to Republic Park, creating a "front porch" for the institution.

Richard Gluckman, David Mayner (principals); Elizabeth Rexrode, Mark Fiedler (project architects); Raffaella Bortoluzzi, Benjamin Checkwitch, Lea Ciavarra, Ching-Loong Tai, William Truitt, Dean Young (design team)

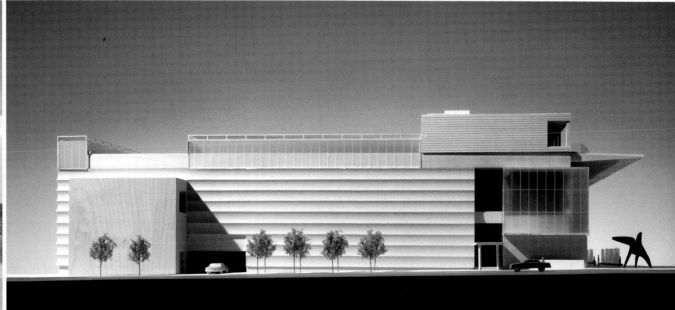

MII AMO SPA
SEDONA, ARIZONA
2001

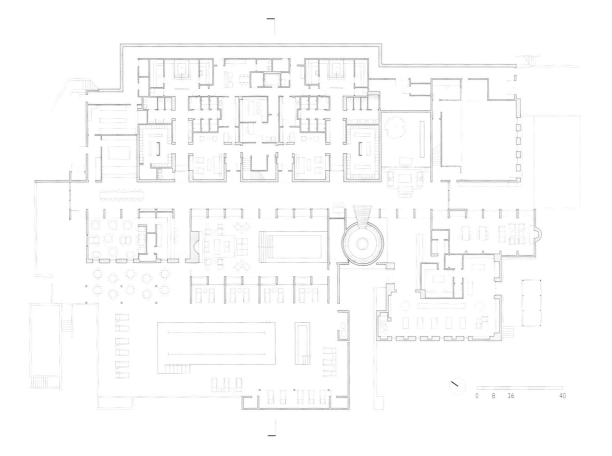

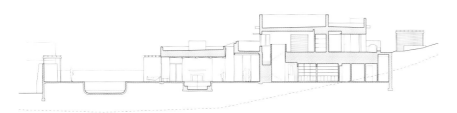

0   8   16   40

Boynton Canyon, a narrow box canyon with
400-foot-high red rock walls, inspired the
design of this spa complex in the Upper Sonoran
Desert. A 172-foot-long circulation spine has a
continuous skylight that illuminates five adobe-
brick towers that echo the traditional masonry
structures of the Southwest. The main floor is
dedicated to public spaces: indoor and outdoor
pools, library, store, gym, and café. The towers
contain private massage rooms and health treatment and relaxation areas.

Natural light and water are essential elements
throughout the spa. The "crystal grotto,"
the symbolic heart of the facility, features an
earthen floor, domed ceiling, and oculus oriented
to the sun's position at the summer solstice. A
stream originating from this space leads visitors
along the entry walkway, then feeds a garden
of native vegetation at the main arrival area.
Six casitas, located amid a grove of cottonwood
trees, are designed around interlocking
landscaped courtyards to maximize privacy
and views.

Richard Gluckman (principal); Dana Tang,
Gregory Yang (project architects); Alex Hurst,
Mark Fiedler, Dean Young, Carolyn Foug,
Julie Torres Moskovitz, Michael Sheridan,
Nina Seirafi, Antonio Palladino (design team)
Associate architect: Marwan Al-Sayed
Architects

MATCHBOX HOUSE
LONG ISLAND, NEW YORK
2001

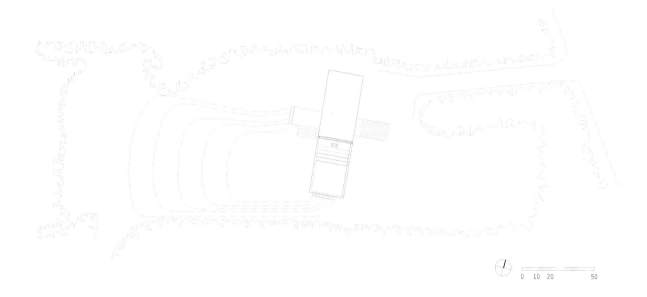

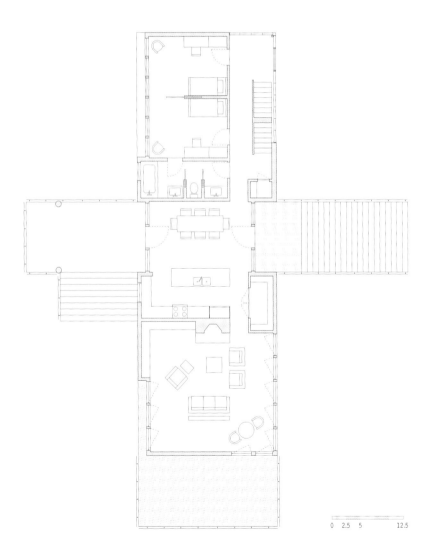

Located on the easternmost tip of Long Island, this 3,600-square-foot weekend house exploits the picturesque landscape of its wetland site. The building is elevated above the flood zone; it is oriented to take advantage of prevailing summer winds and deflect adverse winter winds. The structural strategy incorporates multiple cantilevers of built-up plywood walls. The organizational strategy features an east-west axis defined by the entry stair, which leads through the dining room to the rear yard, and a north-south axis, which climbs to an upper deck that provides a panoramic view to the sea. Economical materials—cedar siding, cement board, and translucent polycarbonate panels—define the spatial volumes within the building's rectangular mass.

Richard Gluckman (principal); David Pysh (project architect); Sarah Dunn, Srdjan Jovanovic Weiss, Michael McClure, Patrick O'Brien, Suzanne Song (design team)

WHITNEY MUSEUM OF
AMERICAN ART EXPANSION
NEW YORK, NEW YORK
2002

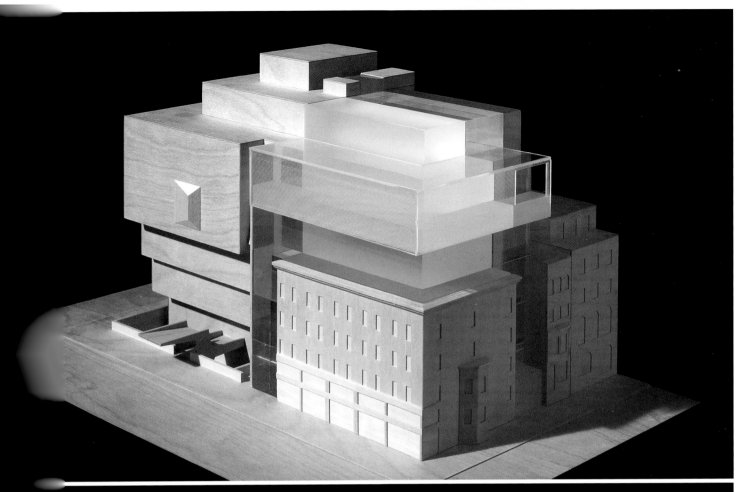

An entry to an invited competition, this proposal expands the Whitney Museum of American Art, previously expanded and renovated by Gluckman Mayner Architects in the 1990s. The 87,000-square-foot addition is the reciprocal of the Whitney's 1966 Breuer building, complementing its weight with a glass-enclosed cantilevered structure housing four levels of coplanar galleries. The addition is inserted behind the facades of brownstone buildings along Madison Avenue; setbacks at the third and fifth floors both respect their scale and introduce natural light into all the new exhibition spaces. Circulation between the new structure and the Breuer building is accommodated by bridges that span the vacated shaft of a large elevator. This vertical shaft counterbalances the strong horizontal axis at each level. Slots within a series of interconnected vertical spaces bring natural light deep into the addition.

Richard Gluckman (principal); Srdjan Jovanovic Weiss (design team)

MORI ARTS CENTER
TOKYO, JAPAN
2003

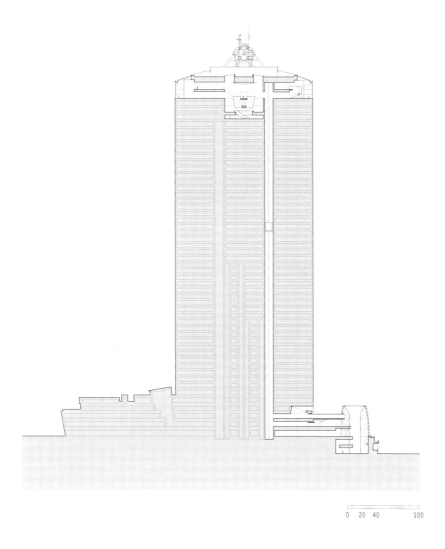

0   20   40   100

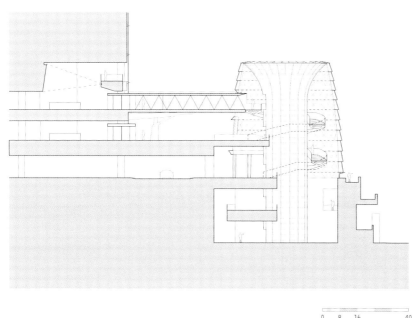

0   8   16   40

This 100,000-square-foot arts center in Roppongi Hills is comprised of two parts. At the base of the office tower, the museum cone, a 100-foot-high glass and steel structure, identifies the cultural component of the commercial development. It connects five floors of public circulation and links the garden with the lower museum lobby. A funnel-shaped concrete core contains elevators and supports the lightweight facade of overlapping fritted-glass "shingles." Coiling between the funnel structure and the facade is a sweeping stair. At night, the museum cone becomes a glowing lantern.

The exhibition venue occupies the top five floors of the 53-story tower. The complex program includes a museum, public observation galleries and promenade, conference center and academy, shop, restaurant-café, art-handling spaces, administrative offices, and private club and restaurant. Four top-lit and three side-lit galleries, which may be subdivided with sliding walls, offer strong, simple volumes oriented with the core of the tower. Two glass-wrapped art and technology galleries, which extend to the edge of the building, allow artists to propose works that address the view and the city beyond. The two-story observation spaces and promenade at the top of the tower set off the orthogonal volumes of the museum from the more complex geometries of the building itself. A dramatic four-story, rough-Indian-sandstone-walled upper atrium provides access to the top floors of the tower.

Richard Gluckman (principal); Sam Brown, Dana Tang (project architects); Eric Chang, Mark Fiedler, Carolyn Foug, Bobby Han, Alex Hurst, Julie Torres Moskovitz, Taro Narahara, Jasmit Rangr, Kaori Sato, Suzanne Song, Anya Bokov, Esther Tsoi (design team)
Mori Tower architect: Kohn Pedersen Fox
Associate architect: Irie Miyake Architects & Engineers

TRIBECA LOFT
NEW YORK, NEW YORK
2003

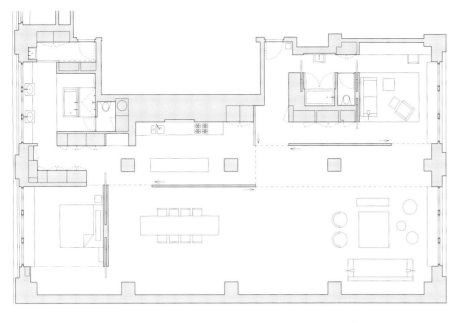

0 2.5 5   12.5

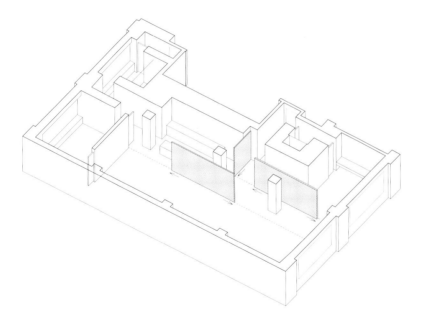

A series of moveable and fixed elements organize this 3,000-square-foot loft for two art collectors. Two large aluminum-framed art walls covered in raw canvas travel nearly the full length of the loft. Translucent plastic walls set perpendicular to the art walls may be configured to create a multitude of formal and informal settings for entertaining, dining, work, and sleep. Enclosed in dark brown, engineered-veneer wood panels on the outside, the bathrooms are on the inside clad in full-height, back-painted glass in vibrant colors. The largest space of the loft is the mutable living/gallery/dining/kitchen. The master bedroom suite may be closed off by sliding walls. The study, separated from the living room and entry by sliding partitions, may be used as a guest room and is adjacent to the guest bath. The varied, mostly monochrome palette of materials includes epoxy terrazzo, tinted plaster, natural canvas, translucent plastic, back-painted glass, reconstituted wood veneer, and aluminum plate.

Richard Gluckman (principal); Gregory Yang (project architect); Ulrike Traut, William Watson, Ching-Loong Tai, Benjamin Checkwitch, Julie Torres Moskovitz, Nina Seirafi (design team)

MUSEO PICASSO MALAGA
MALAGA, SPAIN
2004

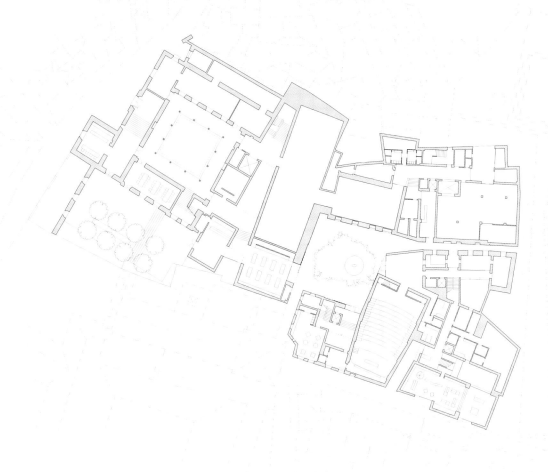

0 10 20   50

Located in the birthplace of Pablo Picasso, this 83,000-square-foot museum complex features a sixteenth-century **palacio** and a matrix of seven renovated and new structures within a historic precinct of the city. The new buildings respect the scale, texture, and articulation of the historic urban fabric; the simple geometric forms, rendered in white plaster, clearly announce a modern intervention. The museum complex is punctuated by a sequence of outdoor spaces that orient visitors and assist them in navigating the museum. The cloistered courtyard of the Palacio de Buenavista, bounded by galleries for the permanent collection, is one such focal point. The Plaza de la Higuera, a new urban space containing an ancient fig tree, is framed by the old and new buildings for the education department, theater, and bookstore.

The principal addition, the structure for changing exhibitions, is mostly concealed behind adjacent buildings. Its simple, undifferentiated face is a foil to the more animated facades surrounding the Plaza de la Higuera. Capping the structure is a plane of aluminum louvers that protect a large skylight and roof patio and act as a detached cornice. The skylight is regulated by internal control devices as well as by a continuous scrim at the ceiling. The historic **toldo**—a fabric stretched over a space to provide shade—influenced the selection of the scrim, which ultimately relied on modern sail-making technology for its construction.

Richard Gluckman (principal); Martin Marciano (project architect); Elena Cannon, Celia Chiang, Srdjan Jovanovic Weiss, Russo Panduro, Amina Razvi, João Regal, Elizabeth Rexrode, Kaori Sato, Nina Seirafi, Tamaki Uchikawa, Thomas Zoli (design team)
Associate architect: Camara/Martin Delgado Arquitectos

SCULPTURE GARDEN
PAVILION
BRIDGEHAMPTON,
NEW YORK
2004

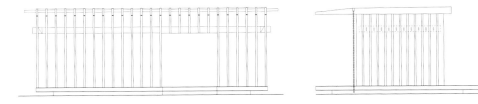

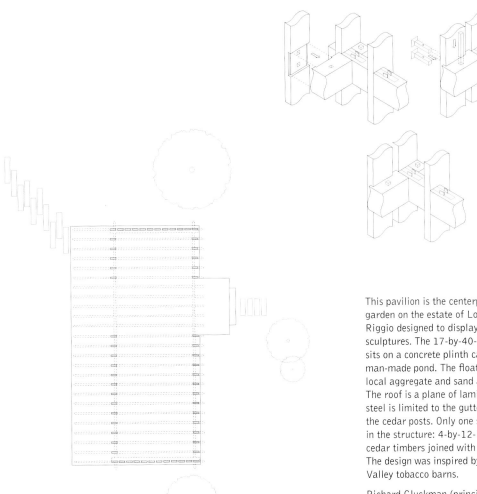

This pavilion is the centerpiece of a private garden on the estate of Louise and Leonard Riggio designed to display Isamu Noguchi sculptures. The 17-by-40-foot open-air structure sits on a concrete plinth cantilevered over a man-made pond. The floating slab is cast with local aggregate and sand and is terrazzo-ground. The roof is a plane of laminated glass. The use of steel is limited to the gutter and the pads under the cedar posts. Only one size of timber was used in the structure: 4-by-12-inch Alaskan yellow cedar timbers joined with mahogany dowels. The design was inspired by Connecticut River Valley tobacco barns.

Richard Gluckman (principal); David Taber (project architect); Georg Thiersch (design team)
Pavilion fabricator: Tom Matthews
Garden designer: Edwina von Gal

0   2.5   5   12.5

MOMA DESIGN AND
BOOK STORES
NEW YORK, NEW YORK
2004

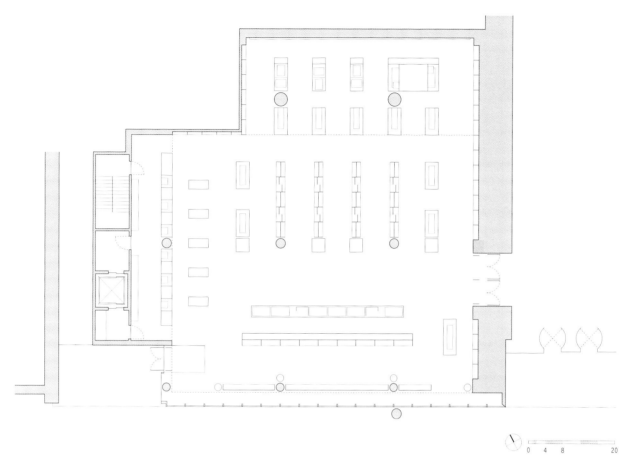

Two distinct retail spaces, each defined by a different palette of materials and colors, demonstrate extraordinary attention to the demands of retail operations in a busy museum setting. The MoMA Design and Book Store occupies 6,400 square feet facing Fifty-third Street. The grid of the curtain wall is extended through the depth of the space, creating a series of zones and terminating in a display wall. Adjacent to the glass facade, high and low walls enclose a narrow book-lined space that establishes a transition between street and store. At the center of the retail space, four tall fixtures that display household objects act as spatial dividers. Lining the outer walls, a modular system of recessed niches with adjustable shelves displays a wide variety of MoMA merchandise.

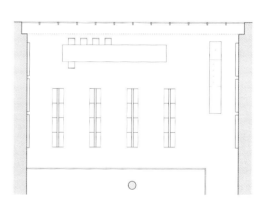

From its position on the second floor of the museum, the 1,600-square-foot MoMA Books overlooks both the main lobby and the historic buildings across Fifty-fourth Street. A suite of furniture constructed of steel plate with a brown-black finish includes three monolithic bookcases as well as wall-mounted shelves, service counter, and reading table. Gluckman Mayner Architects also designed a satellite retail area on the sixth floor.

Richard Gluckman (principal); Sam Brown, Michael Sheridan (project architects); Nancy Choi, Shannon Han, Taro Narahara (design team)

GREEN RESIDENCE
AUSTIN, TEXAS
2005

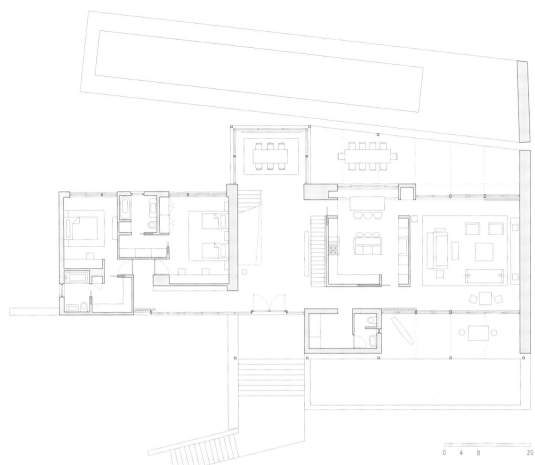

Perched on the edge of a limestone bluff, this three-story, 5,500-square-foot house provides a sense of solitude and seclusion. The west entry facade uses louvers and freestanding walls for privacy and sun protection. Garden walls and a long rectangular reflecting pond define the formal entry. The east facade maximizes close views to a lake formed by the damming of the Colorado River and distant views to the city center. Local requirements dictated an exterior of masonry and natural materials: cleft Texas Lueders limestone, characterized by its materiality and texture, along with stucco and cedar siding, is used for the interior and exterior walls. The interior assigns public and private areas to opposite sides of the entry hall. The master bedroom suite forms a private upper level. Interior living areas flow seamlessly into and out of the garden through large glass doors and windows.

Inside, the material palette consists of limestone, natural wood (oak, mahogany, wenge), blackened steel, glass, and concrete. Blackened steel gives visual weight to the sculptured stair, while translucent and back-painted glass provide a feeling of lightness at the lower-level stair and master bedroom.

Richard Gluckman (principal); Elizabeth Rexrode (project architect); Rachel Doherty, Nina Seirafi, Ching-Loong Tai, Benjamin Checkwitch (design team)

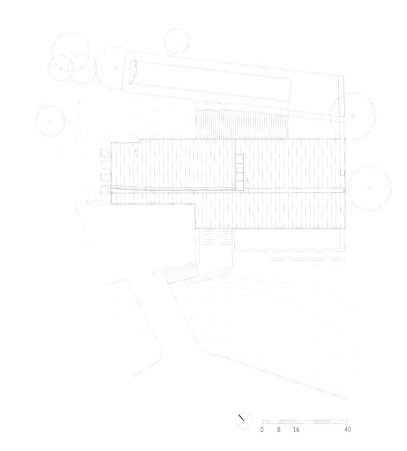

ROBIN HOOD LIBRARY
FOR P.S. 192
NEW YORK, NEW YORK
2005

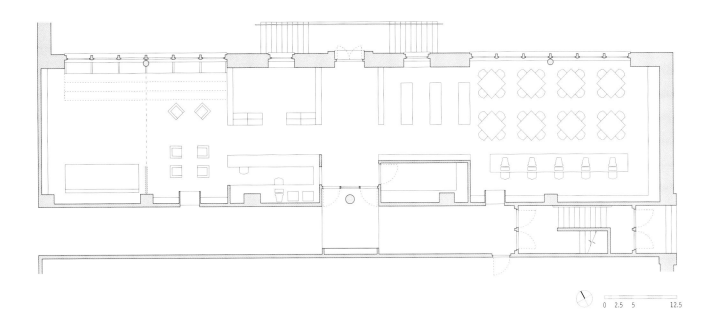

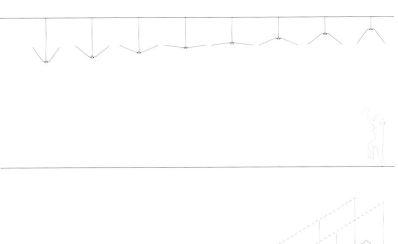

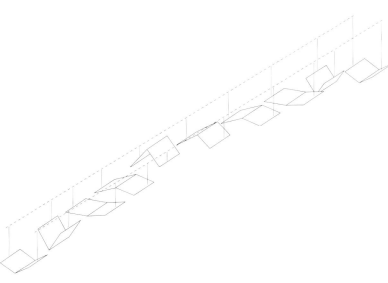

This public elementary school library renovation—one of five executed by Gluckman Mayner Architects—is part of a philanthropic initiative targeting public schools. The program's mission is to transform the libraries into vital resources for the school community as a whole. In response to a tight budget, the design focuses on a select number of signature elements. Light fixtures derived from the photos of Eadweard Muybridge and Etienne-Jules Marey suggest flying books. Distinctive graphics applied to walls and ceilings and wood surrounds complement stock metal shelving and industrial carpeting. The 2,400-square-foot library includes the entry; circulation desk; presentation and free-form reading areas; instructional area, including computer workstations; and storage for book carts and audiovisual equipment.

Under large windows, a long, stepped seat with jewel-colored cushions serves as a day-lit reading area. Casual amphitheater-style seating on the floor is used for readings, lessons, and performances. An adjacent courtyard offers communication with the outdoors. Major materials, including bamboo flooring, formaldehyde-free wheat straw board, and recycled plastic, are child friendly and sustainable.

Richard Gluckman (principal); Dana Tang (project manager); David Taber, Ching-Loong Tai (project architects); John Bellettiere, Okang Hemmings (design team)
Graphic design: 2x4

IGLESIA EVANGELICA
DE CO-OP CITY
BRONX, NEW YORK
2005

113_ IGLESIA EVANGELICA DE CO-OP CITY

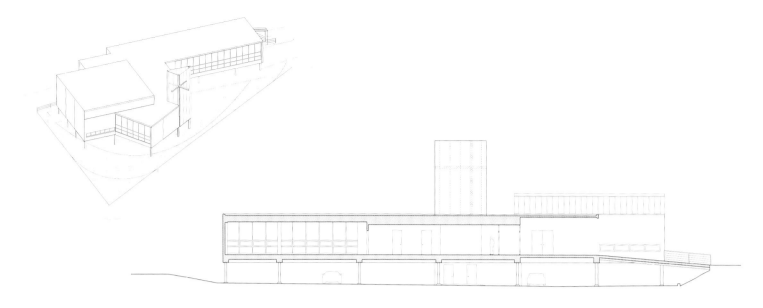

Designed for a dynamic Methodist congregation in the Bronx, this church occupies a challenging site: the buildable area is defined by the intersection of two major highways, and it contains a flood catchment area. The major elements of the program are elevated on one level; the area below provides space for parking and future expansion. The shape of the building conforms to the geometry of the site. The triangular tower and cross—prominent elements visible from the immediate neighborhood of Co-op City and the adjoining highways—mark the building as a place of worship.

The processional movements of celebratory events inform the organization. From the entry, congregants move clockwise to the narthex, through the chapel and into the nave. From the nave, churchgoers exit directly to the porch, completing the cycle. The porch, oriented to the southeast, accommodates gatherings before or after Sunday morning services. A multi-purpose room is used for social functions and after-school programs. The four main interior spaces—sanctuary, chapel, narthex, and multi-purpose room—each have clear architectural identities, while support areas are simple, inexpensive, and functional. The heart of the church, the sanctuary, is a high-ceilinged square room with clerestory windows on two sides. Awning windows close to the floor provide cross-ventilation. The adjacent chapel, separated from the sanctuary by a large sliding wall, provides space for smaller services and more intimate gatherings.

Richard Gluckman (principal); Perry Whidden (project architect); Srdjan Jovanovic Weiss, Jasmit Rangr (design team)

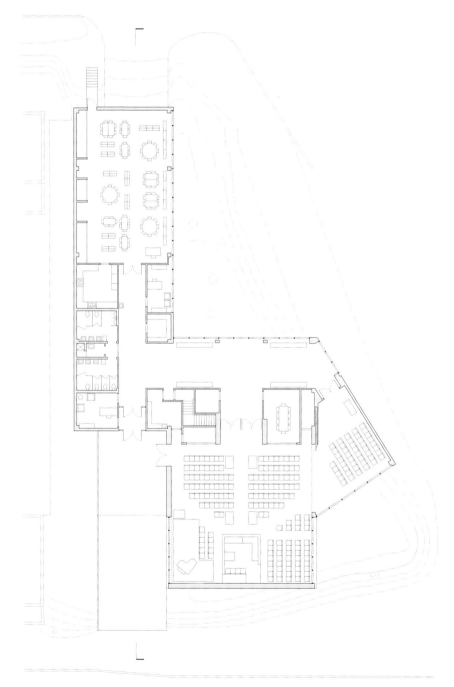

0   5   10   25

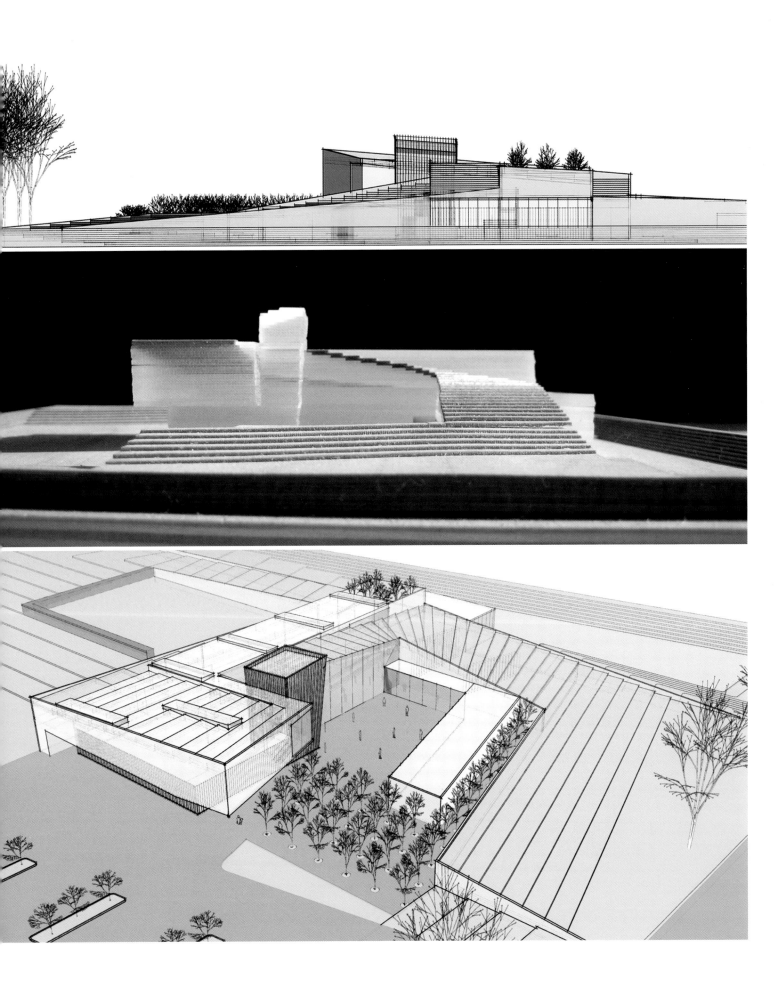

This proposal calls for an 80,000-square-foot museum with exhibition galleries, library, auditorium/lecture hall, educational workshops, and café on a site adjacent to a heavily trafficked highway. The landscape and natural light of the East End of Long Island were significant factors in driving the design. Two spiraling circulation patterns—an interior art path and an exterior landscape path—inspired the form of the building. Both terminate to the southeast: the preeminent orientation of the East End. Partly submerging the building enhances the dialogue between museum and landscape. This strategy also conformed to height restrictions, suppressed the parking area, provided an acoustic buffer to the highway, and referred to the traditional buried potato-storage barns.

Richard Gluckman (principal); Thomas Zoli (design team)

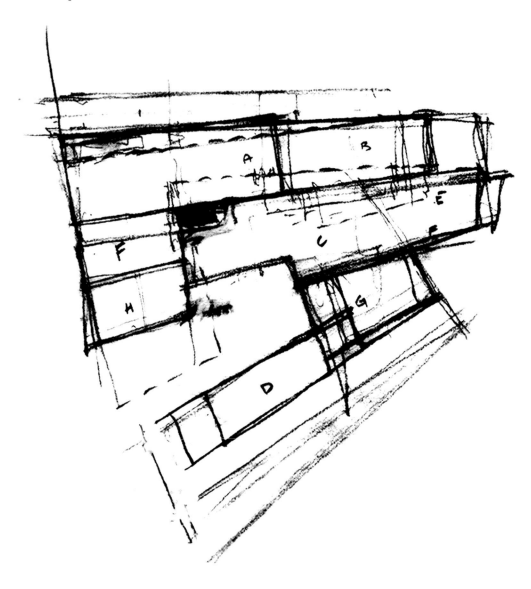

KELLY SHEAR STUDIO
AND ARCHIVES
COLUMBIA COUNTY,
NEW YORK
2005

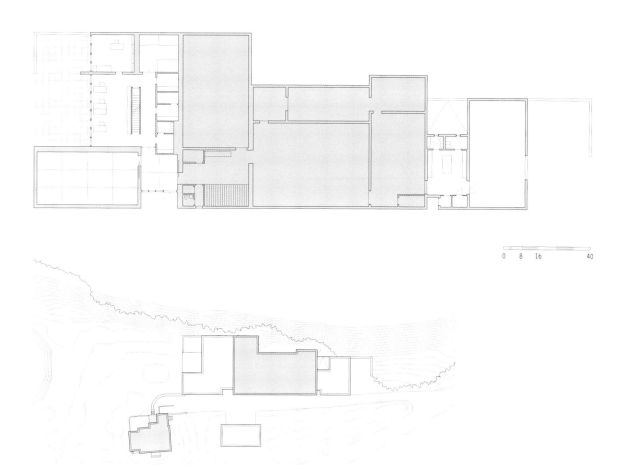

0   8   16   40

0   20   40   100

An expansion of an existing studio building, this 17,500-square-foot group of structures comprises archives, library, offices, viewing gallery, art-handling workshop, and garage. An existing concrete-block wall was extruded to frame the additions, which are constructed of stuccoed concrete. This wall is the reciprocal of the mature grove of pines, planted by the owner thirty years earlier, that defines the entry zone. The simple geometries of the additions derive from the original studio, and the distinct volumes describe interior functions. A patio connects the offices and the landscape, and the only windows are oriented to the pond and woods beyond. An interior stair lined in translucent glass links the archives and offices to a second-floor library. Polycarbonate skylights admit natural light into the studio, library, and art-handling workshop.

Richard Gluckman (principal); Michael Sheridan, Gregory Yang (project architects)

THE WAREHOUSE,
SYRACUSE UNIVERSITY
SYRACUSE, NEW YORK
2006

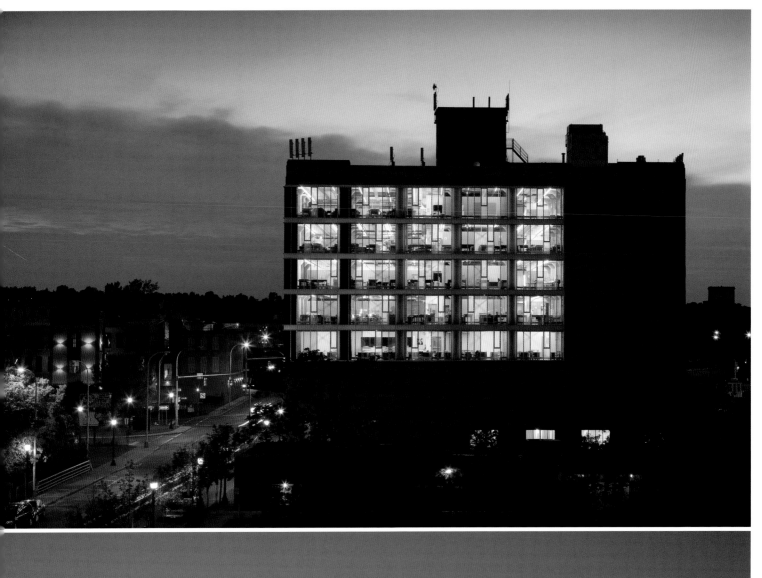

This intervention into a 140,000-square-foot, 1920s warehouse in downtown Syracuse provided the university's School of Architecture with a temporary home and now contains the School of Visual and Performing Arts, community art spaces, and certain programs of the School of Architecture. A significant portion of the existing building skin was replaced with blue, clear, and orange Panelite insulated units that animate the facade. Among the flexible spaces within are studios and classrooms, 125-seat lecture hall, reading room, community and student gallery spaces, café, community and arts incubator spaces, administrative offices, and library storage; the renovation includes new mechanical, electrical, plumbing, and fire protection systems, stairs, and elevators. Respect for the structural frame of the warehouse, and a rigorous application of basic elements, systems, and materials, create a spare and efficient environment. The project proceeded from purchase to occupancy in eleven months.

Richard Gluckman (principal); Martin Marciano (project manager); Sam Brown, Mark Fiedler (project architects); Eunkyung Kim, Patrick Head, Okang Hemmings, Nadia Meratla, Cody Meeks, Thomas Zoli (design team)
Executive architect: V.I.P. Structures, Inc.

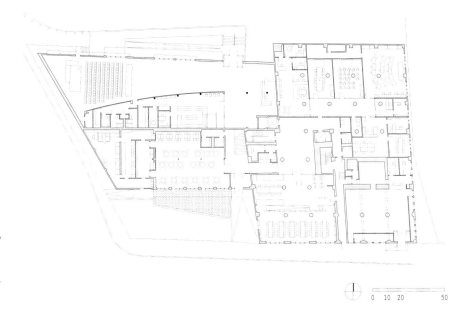

0 10 20   50

KENYON HALL,
VASSAR COLLEGE
POUGHKEEPSIE,
NEW YORK
2006

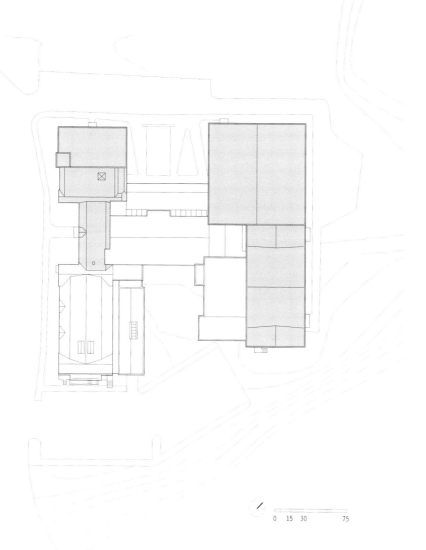

This renovation and expansion of a campus field house provides 75,000 square feet of academic, arts, and athletics spaces. The middle of the original H-shaped building was demolished; an infill structure provides a new front entry, lounge, and six general-purpose classrooms on two floors. Each classroom features a "double horseshoe" design that utilizes two semicircular tiers of seating. A 244-seat dance theater is inserted in the swimming pool; the excavated basin and its great barrel-vaulted ceiling create a dedicated, state-of-the-art dance venue. Stone panels from the old locker and shower rooms were reused on the walls that line the seating platform, and a green-room structure was built nearby. Within the athletics facilities, a new volleyball gymnasium, competition-quality squash courts, and expanded locker rooms replace obsolete handball courts.

David Mayner (principal); Michael Hamilton (project manager); William Watson, Elena Cannon, Ching-Loong Tai, Taro Narahara, Tom Houston (design team)

0 15 30   75

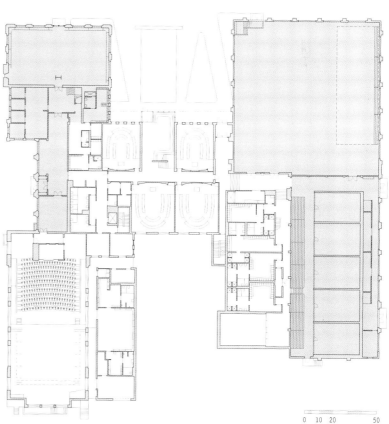

0 10 20   50

ONE KENMARE SQUARE
NEW YORK, NEW YORK
2006

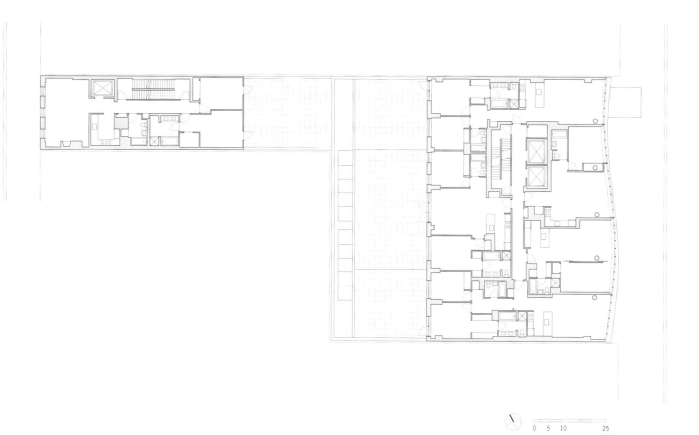

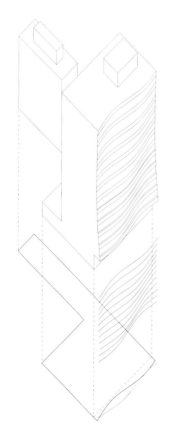

This 86,000-square-foot condominium consists of an eleven-story volume on Lafayette Street and a six-story volume on Crosby Street. The curved facade, generated by a sine wave, shifts north and west at each level, approximating the rippling effect of a flag. The facade gradually slides behind the street setback line, maintaining an unbroken surface. The segmented shape of each floor slab is identical, which simplified construction and reduced cost. Large ribbon windows provide generous light and unobstructed views; together with bands of textured iridescent gray brick, they animate the facade with changing shadows throughout the day. A deep notch on the north and south facades divides the building; this split, emphasized by a change of materials, improves the proportions of the overall mass.

Richard Gluckman (principal); Dana Tang (project manager); James Lim (project architect); Sima Rustom (design team)
Architect of record: H. Thomas O'Hara Architect

CENTRAL PARK SOUTH
RESIDENCE
NEW YORK, NEW YORK
2006

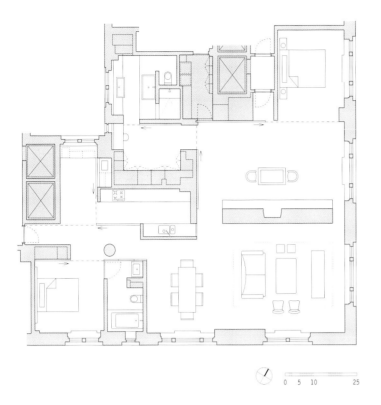

0 5 10   25

This 2,200-square-foot apartment combines two smaller units to create a pied-à-terre for a couple with a collection of photography and paintings. The living area, master bedroom, and adjoining study enjoy unobstructed views of Central Park to the north. Pastel sliding walls are used to reconfigure and screen different spaces: master bedroom, kitchen, bike room, and guest room. The master bathroom is finished with stone mosaic tiles and features a soaking tub of Japanese hinoki.

Richard Gluckman (principal); Martin Marciano (project architect); Gregory Yang, Jenny Wu, Kaori Sato, Nina Seirafi, Brian Salek (design team)

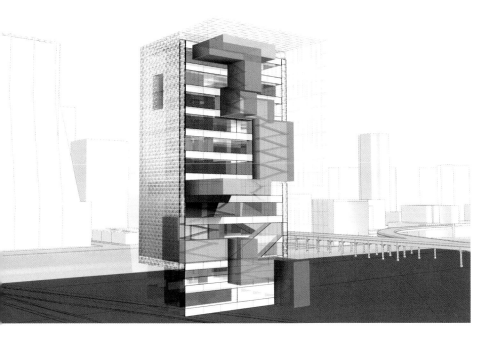

This design study, presented in "The Guggenheim: Architecture" exhibition, proposes a 480,000-square-foot, industrially sized museum complex for a site in the rail yards adjacent to the High Line. Two hundred feet square, the building has ten levels above the ground and two levels below. Ten semi-autonomous exhibition venues occupy the structure, each on its own level. Escalators connect the street and the High Line to the fourth floor, where individual elevators distribute visitors to the different floors. Interstitial spaces accommodate all mechanical and support services. The components are linked by a vertical "street" that provides a slow path through each level. A double skin—glass on the exterior and polycarbonate on the interior—regulates and diffuses light, permits natural ventilation, and creates a buffer for the highly controlled interior spaces. The skin is mutable: transparent, translucent, and opaque, it works in concert with the building's luminous qualities to elicit an ambiguity of form and use.

Richard Gluckman (principal); Thomas Zoli, Ryan Harvey, James Henry (design team)

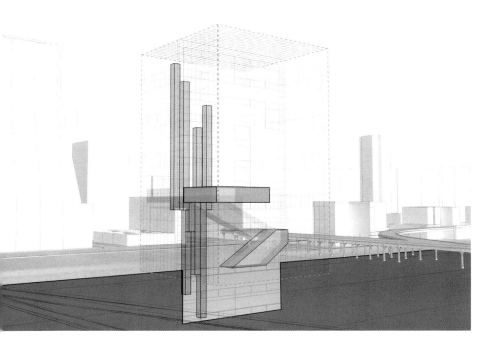

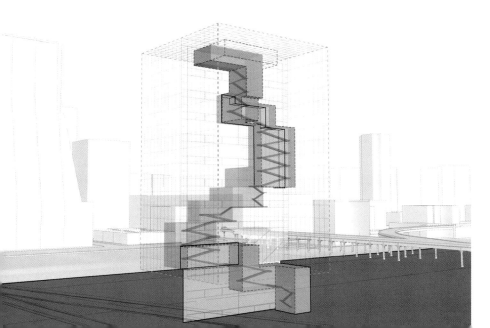

GAGOSIAN GALLERY
TWENTY-FIRST STREET
NEW YORK, NEW YORK
2006

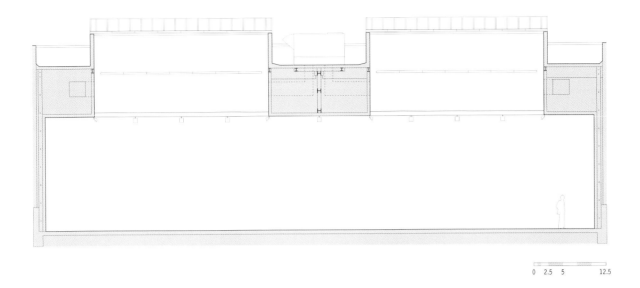

0   2.5   5   12.5

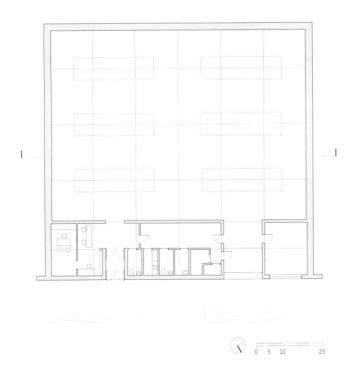

0   5   10   25

This new 6,000-square-foot exhibition building supplements the client's main gallery three blocks away. Inexpensive materials—concrete, brick, plastic, and gypsum board—continue the precedents established at the main space. The gallery is reduced to its primary components: scale, proportion, light, and frame.

Richard Gluckman (principal); Thomas Zoli (project architect); Tara Bremer, Ryan Harvey, Okang Hemmings, Miguel Bao (design team)

MUSEUM OF
CONTEMPORARY ART
SAN DIEGO
SAN DIEGO, CALIFORNIA
2007

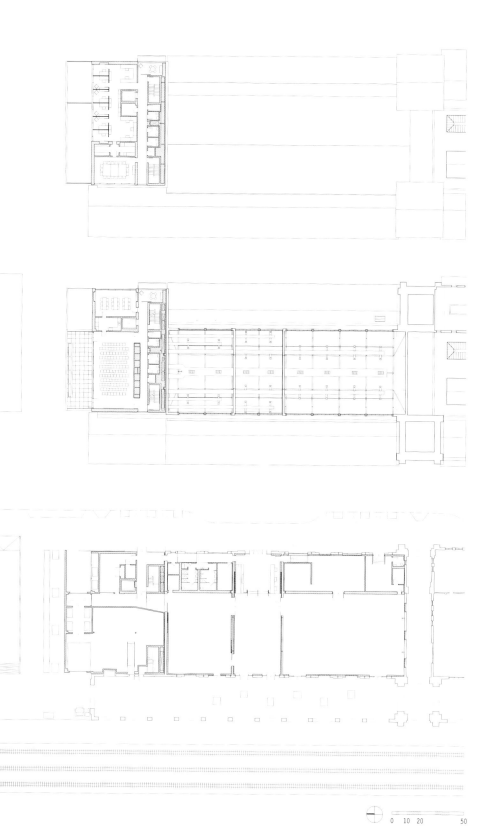

This satellite of the La Jolla–based museum establishes the institution's presence in downtown San Diego. Located in the baggage building of the Santa Fe Railroad terminal, built in 1917, this complex includes the 13,680-square-foot existing structure and an adjacent 13,750-square-foot addition. Both neighbor the passenger terminal and active railroad platforms to the west. The baggage building, with a heavy, Mission-style skin of clay tiles and stucco, was seismically upgraded and restored. The original innovative steel frame and clerestories were left exposed and complemented with carefully integrated mechanical systems, new finishes, and concrete floor. This space is used as a large-scale venue for changing exhibitions and public events.

The three-story addition inverts the language of the original structure. Comprised of a checkerboard of steel, concrete, and channel glass, the facade reveals the offices, studios, and support facilities within. The corrugated panels recall the scale and color of the clay roofing tiles as well as the nature of boxcar construction. Jenny Holzer collaborated on the "sign" cantilevered from the facade. A Richard Serra installation in the arcade, **Santa Fe Depot**, faces the train platforms. Other commissions include permanent installations by Roman de Salvo and Richard Wright.

Richard Gluckman (principal); Robert White (project manager); James Counts (project architect); Robert Edmonds, Benjamin Checkwitch, Dean Young, Srdjan Jovanovic Weiss (design team)
Associate architect: Heritage Architecture & Planning

0 10 20 50

ALBRIGHT-KNOX ART GALLERY
BUFFALO, NEW YORK
2007

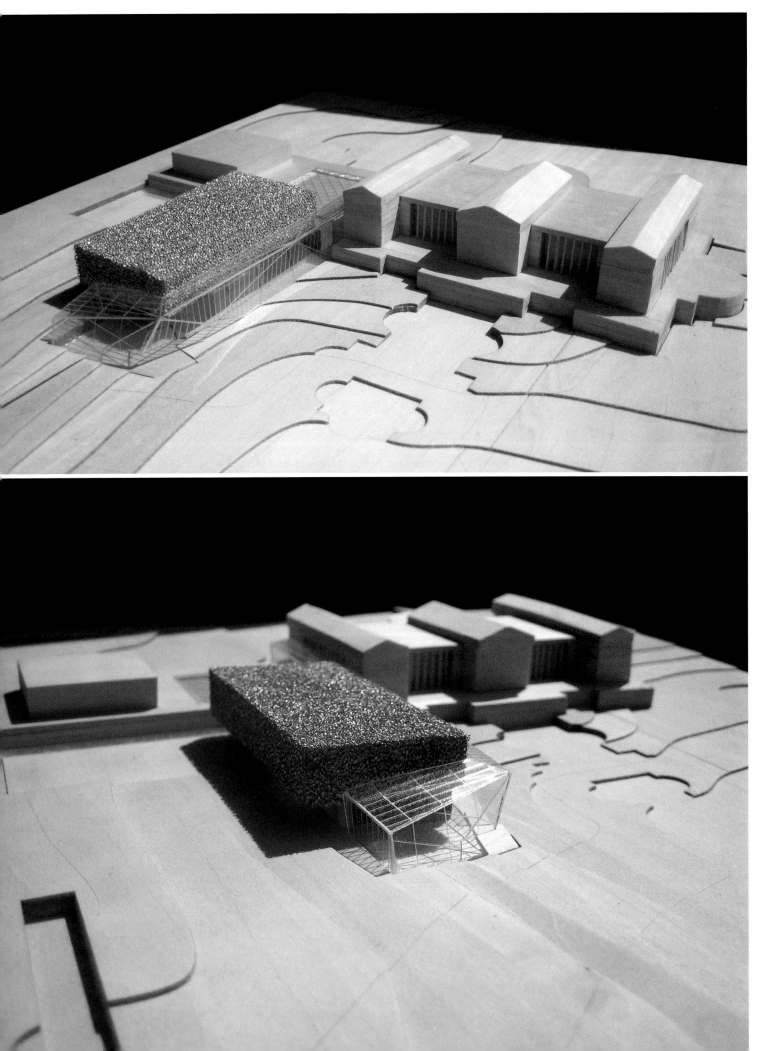

This design study proposes a 42,000-square-foot addition to the museum's Elmwood Avenue campus, which consists of a 1905 Beaux-Arts building designed by E. B. Green and a 1962 modernist addition designed by Gordon Bunshaft. A solid rectangular volume for exhibition galleries, partially wrapped in a glass enclosure, connects to the south side of the 1905 building and its main-level galleries. The new glass galleria connects exhibition areas; develops new public spaces, including café and event space; reorganizes circulation; and creates an observation point with views of the original building's classical facade and a panoramic perspective overlooking Hoyt Lake and the Olmsted-designed Delaware Park to the east. The expansion transforms the existing courtyard into a sky-lit sculpture court and lobby that clarifies circulation in the new complex.

Richard Gluckman (principal); Taylor Aikin, Ryan Harvey (design team)

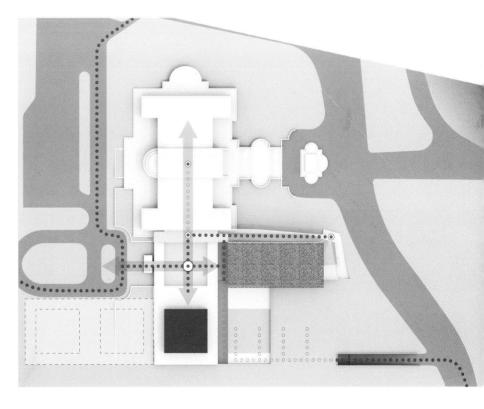

MOMA DESIGN STORE
TOKYO, JAPAN
2007

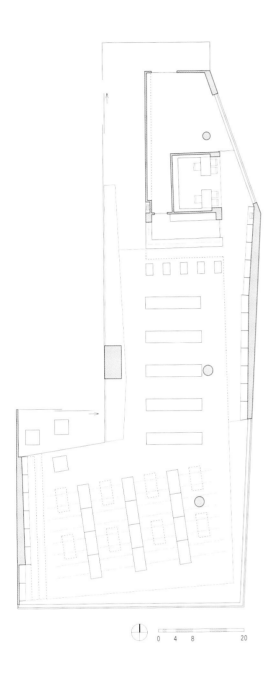

Located in a complex of luxury boutiques in Tokyo's Omotesando district, this 4,500-square-foot design store derives its organization from the "swirl" concept of the base building. Two zones of retail space—one for tall fixtures and the other a field of low fixtures mounted on tracks—allow flexibility in layout. A bold aluminum volume forms the cashier area and isolates storage and a salon for wedding gifts. Environmental graphics—a moiré printed on glass—run throughout the store. The material palette is limited to epoxy terrazzo, aluminum, painted steel, and Corian.

Richard Gluckman (principal); Edowa Shimizu (project architect); Doel Fresse, Eunkyung Kim (design team)
GYRE Building architect: MVRDV
Environmental graphics: 2x4
Associate architect: Nomura Co., Ltd.

```
0   4   8          20
```

PERELMAN BUILDING,
PHILADELPHIA MUSEUM
OF ART
PHILADELPHIA,
PENNSYLVANIA
2007

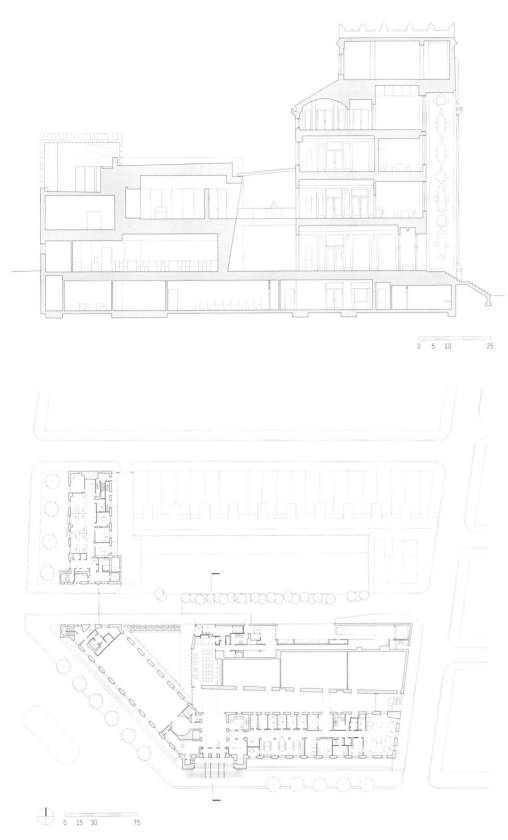

Sited on a two-acre parcel at the edge of Fairmount Park and across Benjamin Franklin Parkway from the museum's main building, this expansion comprises a renovated 100,000-square-foot Art Deco office building and a 60,000-square-foot addition. The landmark exterior and certain interiors of the existing building have been carefully preserved and restored; the addition mediates the change between the institutional scale along the parkway and the small scale of the adjacent residential neighborhood. The complex accommodates all the components of a stand-alone museum: galleries, event spaces, library, archives, café, store, conservation labs, curatorial spaces, offices, storage, and administration.

The addition is organized into three distinct "bars" running east to west. The first is a public sky-lit galleria between the existing building and the new structure; it serves as both exhibition and event space. Within the addition, the second bar accommodates exhibition galleries on the main level and study storage on the upper level. The third bar houses support functions and mechanical spaces. Each bar is expressed using different materials and forms. The galleria is framed by the rear facade of the existing building and the warped masonry wall of the addition, which pitches out six feet at the entry and gradually returns to a plumb wall at the far end. The warp and the irregular surface of the masonry diffuse sunlight, controlling the transition from light to dark, from public areas to light-sensitive galleries. Four layered facades wrap the complex inside and out: the monumental limestone of the original building facing the parkway; the elegant and utilitarian yellow brick of its rear face; the textured concrete brick of the warped wall; and the ground-face concrete block of the north side.

Richard Gluckman, David Mayner (principals); Perry Whidden (project manager); Tom Houston, Dean Young (project architects); Mark Fiedler, Robert Edmonds, Julie Torres Moskovitz, Amina Razvi, James Lee Dyson, Emily Wilson, Carol Chang, Kerry Nolan, Dana Tang (design team)
Preservation architect: Kelly/Maiello Architects & Planners

BRANT FOUNDATION ART
STUDY CENTER
GREENWICH, CONNECTICUT
2008

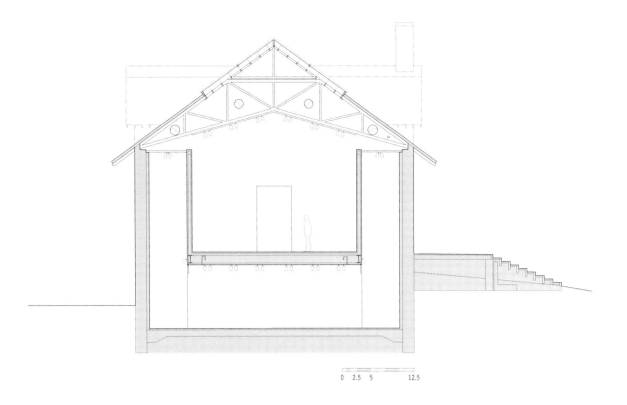

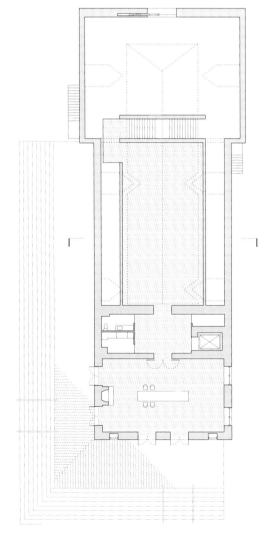

This 9,800-square-foot conversion transforms a stone barn (built in 1902 and substantially rebuilt and expanded as a sports facility in the 1980s) into an art study center for a private foundation. Three galleries, each with distinct spatial characteristics, are inserted into the historic structure. A slot between the new mezzanine gallery and the existing walls allows light to penetrate deep into the building, distinguishing the intervention from the original structure. The "club room" is transformed into a library and exhibition space that retains some of the earlier details of the building. A new skylight is carefully inserted over the wood trusses from the previous renovation.

Richard Gluckman (principal); Melissa Cicetti (project architect); Jonathan Walston (design team)

FUNDACIO SORIGUE
LLEIDA, SPAIN
2008

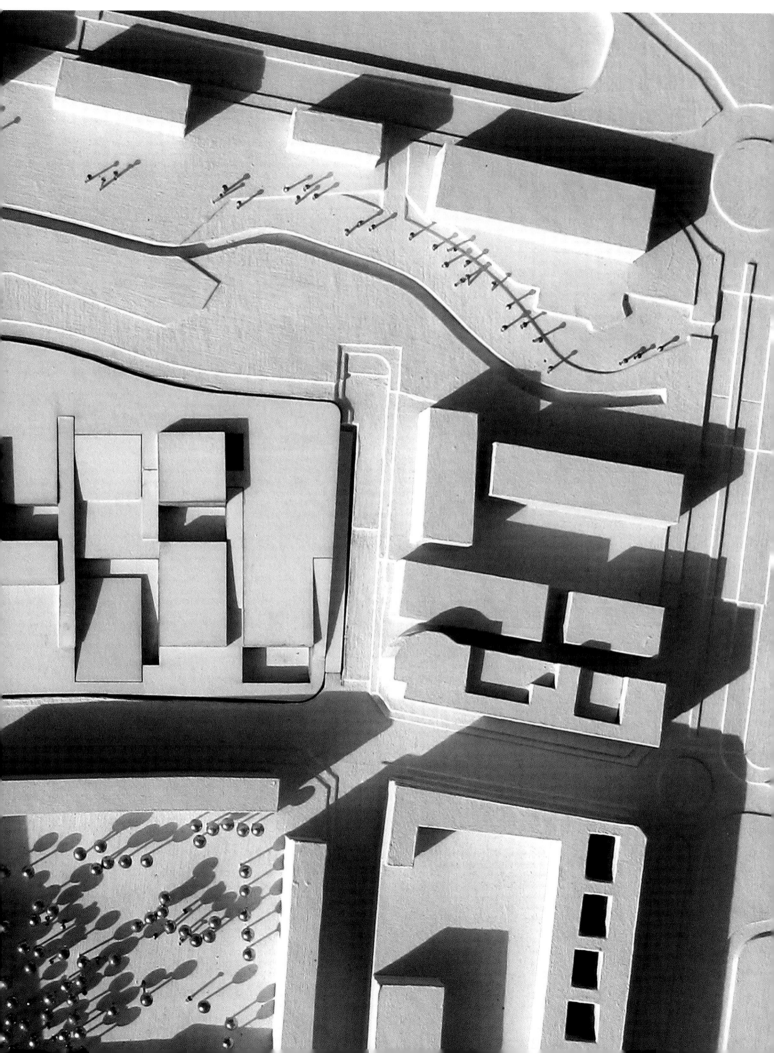

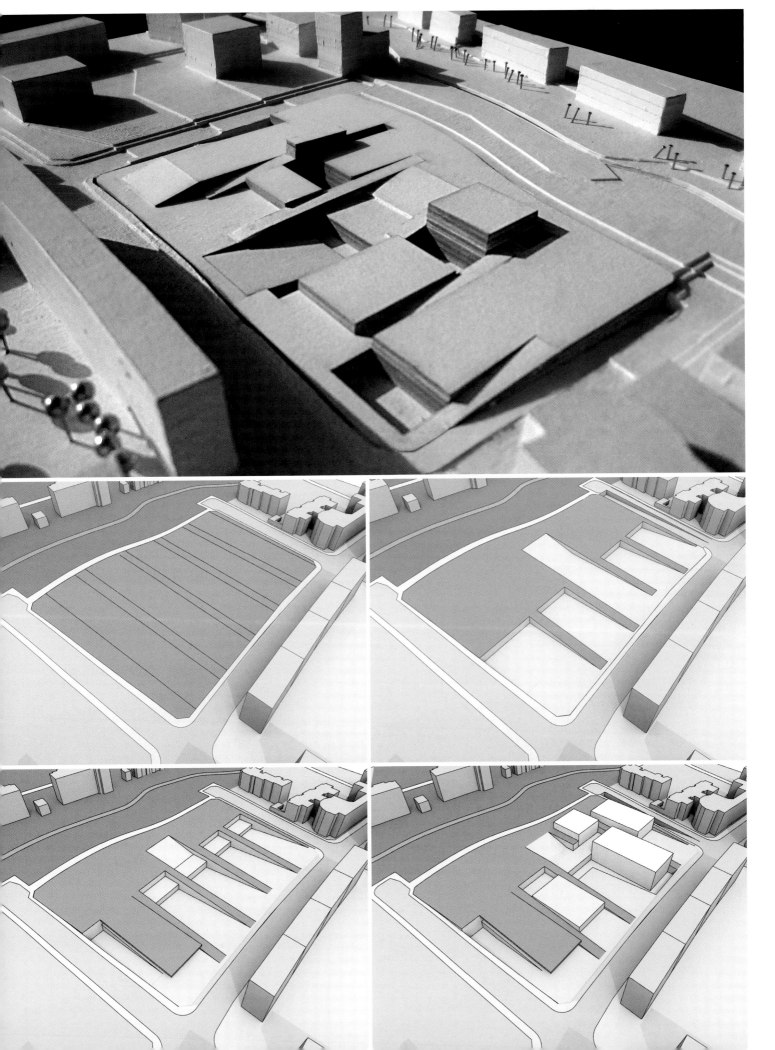

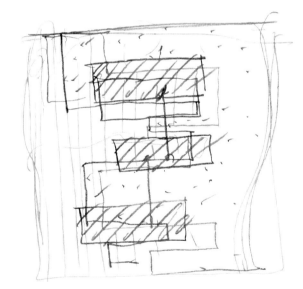

This project integrates a 70,000-square-foot exhibition facility into the landscape to create a museum within a garden. Local precedents—land forms, man-made interventions, and fortifications—informed the cut-and-fill approach of the design. A below-grade, north-south core spine is overlaid with east-west "cuts" of circulation; two open-air patios that serve as interior courtyards interrupt the excavated spine. The open courts admit light and air into the museum and provide orientation points to ease navigation. The southern patio serves the educational, administrative, retail, and art-handling spaces; the northern patio is located at the intersection of the exhibition and event spaces. Distinct circulation paths serve the loading and art-handling areas at the south end of the site and the public facilities at the north end, including the entrance for visitors arriving by car. The pedestrian entrance, a wide ramp from the street, arrives at the main spine at a point between the patios. As visitors approach the site, the building is revealed in an incidental way. This strategy gives prominence to the exterior public spaces; the museum itself is both building and landscape

Richard Gluckman (principal); Cornelia Wu, Filipa Tomaz (project architects); Taylor Aikin, Doel Fresse, Ryan Harvey, Michael Vanreusel, Soohyun Park (design team)

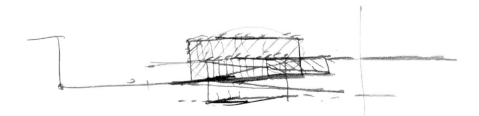

ZHEJIANG UNIVERSITY
MUSEUM OF ART AND
ARCHAEOLOGY
HANGZHOU, CHINA
IN PROGRESS

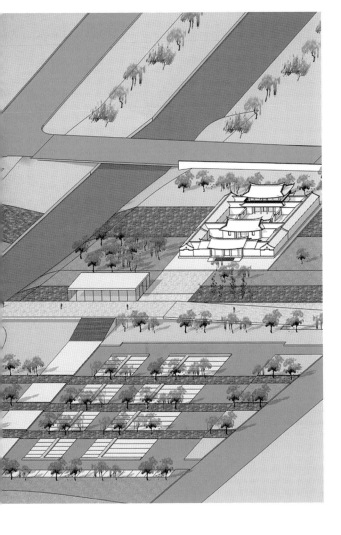

Located in the provincial capital of Hangzhou in southeastern China, this comprehensive teaching museum supports research and study of the arts on a growing university campus. Hangzhou's reputation as a place of serene beauty with dramatic water courses and contemplative landscapes dates to antiquity. The 165,000-square-foot museum, contemporary in aesthetic and function, alludes to various aspects of traditional Chinese architecture and garden design. The complex brings together three major elements—public venues, art study storage, and academics—integrating them with a matrix of courtyards, water features, and borrowed landscape.

The public spaces of the museum are located at the southern and western edges of the building, which draws visitors along a waterside entry path to the main entry courtyard and grand lobby space. The lobby, a double-height interior promenade, looks out to a water garden set in a courtyard. The western end of the lobby leads to galleries for the permanent collection and changing exhibitions and amenities including a café, retail store, and coatroom. Controlled points of connection integrate the museum with the art-handling and storage spaces at the northwest corner and the academic facilities at the northeast corner. The academic area has its own entry and comprises a library, auditorium, classrooms, seminar rooms, study centers, conservation lab, and dedicated education center to support the museum's public outreach.

Richard Gluckman (principal); Dana Tang (project manager); James Lim (project architect); Eunkyung Kim, Tao Liu, So-Hyun Han, Dale Lunan (design team)

CONTEMPORARY ART MUSEUM OF THE PRESIDIO
SAN FRANCISCO, CALIFORNIA
2008

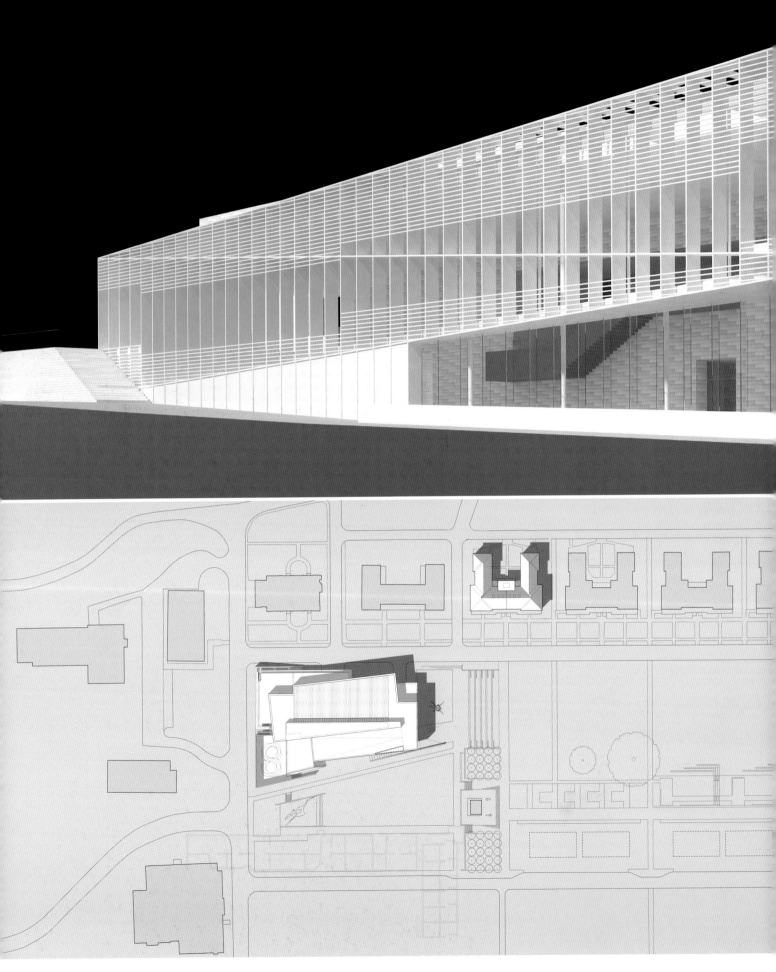

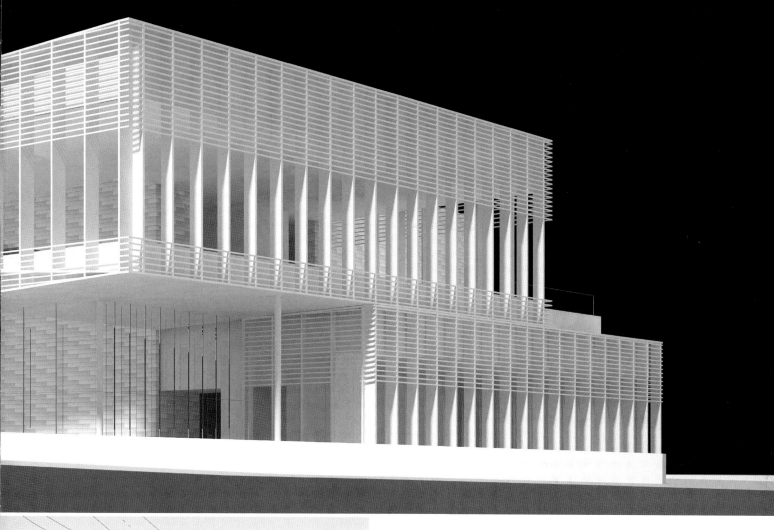

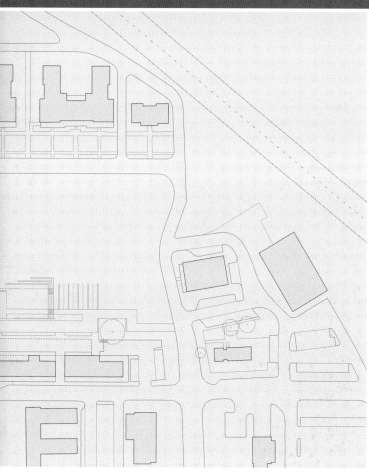

0 30 60   150

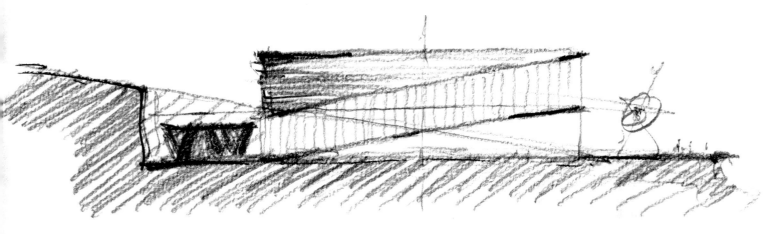

comp '07

Doris and Don Fisher commissioned this 100,000-square-foot museum to house their extensive collection of contemporary art. The site is at the head of the Main Post in the Presidio, a former military base now under the jurisdiction of the Presidio Trust. The museum was intended to energize and transform the Post, providing a catalyst for development that would sustain and preserve its historic landscape and structures as it evolves into a park.

The accessible and inclusive institution would provide exhibition venues, educational facilities, and a great public "living room" for the Presidio. The design of the building is a direct response to the topography of the sloping site, which is located at the hinge between the rigid orthogonal grid of the Main Post and the natural contours of the hills to the south. The design also responds to the historic topography of the Main Post, synthesizing 200 years of architectural styles in a "building of its time" both distinct from and compatible with the styles, textures, scales, materialities, and colors of the existing buildings. The geometry of the historic roadways of the Post and the 25-foot grade change of the site generate an array of slightly splayed volumes. The articulation of the glazed facades is derived from the enclosed porch fronts of the adjacent barracks buildings, and the staggered white masonry of the solid walls refers to the varied use of masonry throughout the Post. The simple color palette unifies the diverse existing structures.

Richard Gluckman (principal); Perry Whidden (project manager); Robert White (project architect); Ryan Harvey, Edowa Shimizu, Wayne Norbeck, Brandon Sanchez, Michael Vanreusel, Phil Gleason (design team)
Associate architect: WRNS Studio

SAADIYAT TEMPORARY CULTURAL PARK
ABU DHABI, UNITED ARAB EMIRATES
IN PROGRESS

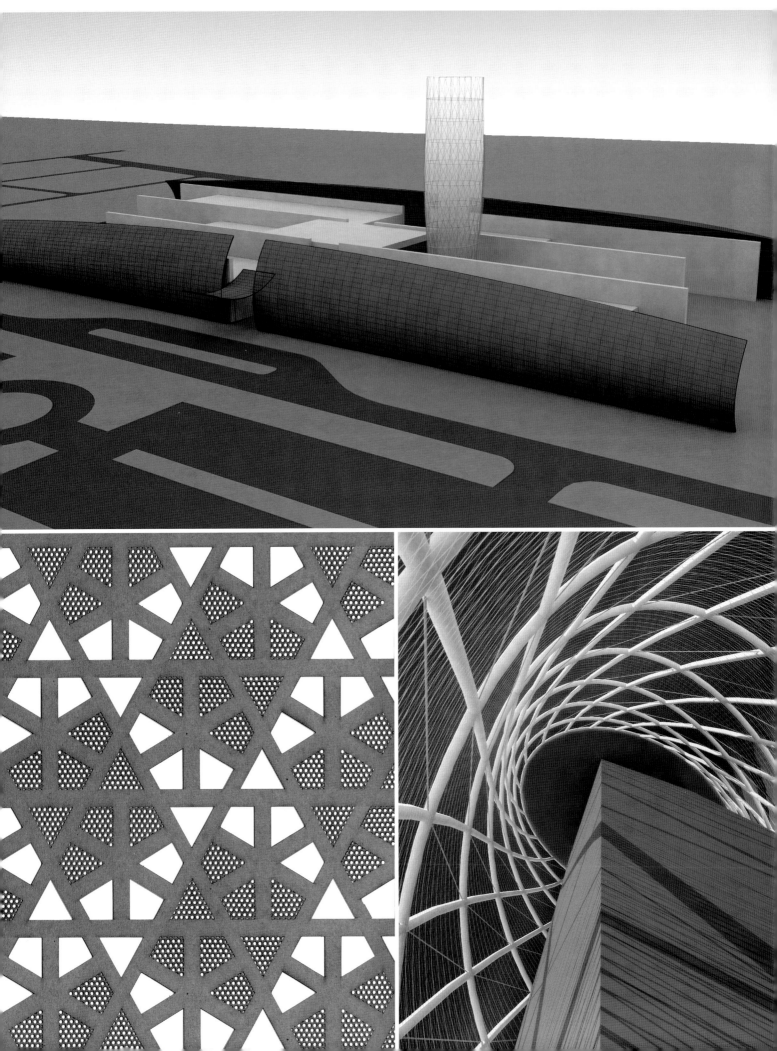

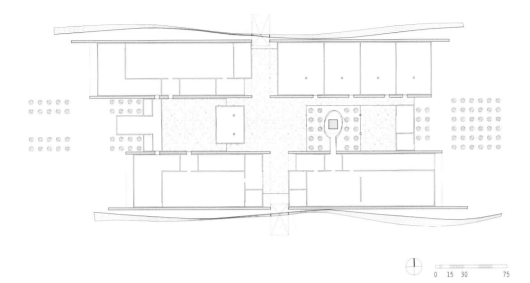

0   15   30   75

This temporary exhibition facility of 180,000 square feet is to be the first building constructed on Saadiyat Island, a major development project in Abu Dhabi. Components include display space for the Louvre and the Guggenheim, providing opportunities for exhibition programs while the permanent buildings are under construction. The facility will also contain the Experience Center, a showcase for the developer.

The simple construction system—a steel frame and long-span trusses for the sawtooth sky-lights—allows for rapid construction and future flexibility. The two signature elements of the building, the observation tower and the facade, are generated by simple geometric manipulations. The tower is a rotated ellipse with a cable-net structure. The facade is based on a pivoted sine wave that allows straight structural members to describe a warped wall. The design of the copper-clad wall refers to the plywood hoarding screens ubiquitous at construction sites throughout the Emirates.

Richard Gluckman, David Mayner (principals); Robert White, Kerry Nolan (project architects); Wayne Norbeck, James Lim, Edowa Shimizu, Phil Gleason, Dale Lunan (design team)

Gluckman Mayner Architects has established a distinguished reputation for its rigorous approach to design and construction. Founded in New York City in 1977, the office has designed a wide range of institutional, commercial, and residential projects throughout the United States, Europe, and Asia. A major component of the firm's practice has been the design of art-related facilities. Gluckman Mayner Architects has received numerous awards from the American Institute of Architects, and in 2005 Richard Gluckman received the National Design Award from the Cooper-Hewitt, National Design Museum.

Richard Gluckman FAIA received his bachelor of architecture and master of architecture degrees from Syracuse University. He has been a visiting critic at the Graduate School of Design at Harvard University, Syracuse University, and Parsons School of Design. David Mayner, who has worked with Richard Gluckman since 1980, was named principal in 1998. He received a master of architecture degree from the Massachusetts Institute of Technology and also holds bachelor of science in mechanical engineering and bachelor of science in art and design degrees from M.I.T.

2000–2009

Richard Gluckman
David Mayner

Richard Aeck
Taylor Aikin
Emily Atwood
Miguel Bao
Sara Bayer
Isabelle Bedard
John Bellettiere
Edgar Bocanegra
Anya Bokov
Raffaella Bortoluzzi
Stefanie Brechbuehler
Tara Bremer
Sam Brown
Melinda Buie
Elena Cannon
Carol Chang
Edgar Garcia Chavez
Benjamin Checkwitch
Rebecca Cheng
Celia Chiang
Nancy Choi
Wilmay Choy
Melissa Cicetti
Hillary Collins
James Counts
Rachel Doherty
Bethune D'Souza
James Lee Dyson
Robert Edmonds
Eugene Eng
Mark Fiedler
Serena Fong
Carolyn Foug
Doel Fresse
Anna Frey
Daniel Gallagher

Phil Gleason
Jessica Goethals
Anna Goldberg
Michael Hamilton
Shannon Han
So-hyun Han
Ryan Harvey
Patrick Head
Okang Hemmings
James Henry
Zack Hinchliffe
Erin Hiser
Tom Houston
Lana Hum
William Hung
Purvi Khant
Eunkyung Kim
John Kim
Karen Kriegel
John LaMonica
Christien Lauro
Christopher Leong
Jennifer Leung
James Lim
Tao Liu
Janly Lo
Jason Long
Ken Louie
Sarah Ludington
Dale Lunan
Dana Maisel
Martin Marciano
Alicia Marvan
Jane McNichol
Cody Meeks
Nadia Meratla
Julie Torres Moskovitz
Taro Narahara
Willa Ng

Pamela Niskanen
Wayne Norbeck
Kerry Nolan
Whitney Odell
Erica Pajerowski
Russo Panduro
Iona Park
Soohyun Park
Jasmit Rangr
Amina Razvi
João Regal
Jennifer Retzer
Elizabeth Rexrode
Mark Rhoads
Jane Riccobono
Encarnita Rivera
Daniel Roldan
Daniella Rossi
Sima Rustom
Brian Salek
Brandon Sanchez
Kaori Sato
Meredith Schweig
Nina Seirafi
Seth Sharp
Noah Shepherd
Michael Sheridan
Edowa Shimizu
Jane Stageberg
Alexander Stolz
Irene Sunwoo
Ching-Loong Tai
David Taber
Dana Tang
Georg Thiersch
Brett Tipert
Richard Tobias
Filipa Tomaz
Ulrike Traut

William Truitt
Esther Tsoi
Tamaki Uchikawa
Cody Umans
Celeste Umpierre
Yolanda Uribe-Plata
Amy Vanderwall
Michael Vanreusel
Jonathan Walston
Scott Watson
William Watson
Lindsay Weiss
Srdjan Jovanovic Weiss
Perry Whidden
Robert White
Amber Wiley
Danielle Wilmot
Emily Wilson
Christian Wofford
Cornelia Wu
Jenny Wu
Gregory Yang
Elise Youn
Dean Young
Susan Yun
Fidel Zabik
Roxie Zeek
Thomas Zoli

Denotes current employee

PROJECT LIST 2000–2009

2000
Mary Boone Gallery Chelsea, New York, New York
Charles Cowles Gallery, New York, New York
Gagosian Gallery Twenty-fourth Street, New York, New York
Gordon Residence III, Southold, New York
Henry Residence, New York, New York
Helmut Lang Department Store Boutiques, Hong Kong, Singapore,
    Taipei, Tokyo, Kobe, Seoul, London, Paris, Manhasset, and New York,
    New York
Helmut Lang Residence, Amagansett, New York
National Design Triennial Exhibition, Cooper-Hewitt, New York,
    New York
Oeri/Bodenmann Residence, New York, New York
Philadelphia Museum of Art Contemporary Galleries, Philadelphia,
    Pennsylvania
Yves Saint Laurent St.-Sulpice, Paris, France
SITE Santa Fe II (project), Santa Fe, New Mexico

2001
Austin Museum of Art (project), Austin, Texas
Peter Blake House (project), Montauk, New York
Cheim and Read Gallery, New York, New York
Salvador Dalí Museum (project), St. Petersburg, Florida
Eyebeam Atelier (proposal), New York, New York
Gap Galleries 2 Folsom, San Francisco, California
Gluckman Mayner Architects Offices, New York, New York
Jenny Holzer Wiesbaden Memorial (project), Wiesbaden, Germany
Helmut Lang 80 Greene Offices, New York, New York
Helmut Lang Aoyama (project), Tokyo, Japan
Helmut Lang Parfumerie, New York, New York, and Frankfurt, Germany
Helmut Lang Residence, New York, New York
Matchbox House, Long Island, New York
Mii amo Spa, Sedona, Arizona
O'Keeffe Research Center, Santa Fe, New Mexico
Pinault Residence, New York, New York

2002
Artist's Warehouse, Brooklyn, New York
Sandra Brant Residence, Montauk, New York
Dallas Museum of Art Expansion (project), Dallas, Texas
GARDE/Untitled Shops Prototype, Tokyo, Japan
Goode Residence (project), New York, New York
House at Sagaponac (project), Sagaponac, New York
Helmut Lang 142 Greene Offices, New York, New York
A New World Trade Center Exhibition, New York, New York,
    and Washington, D.C.
Will Ryman Residence, New York, New York
Whitney Museum of American Art Expansion (project), New York,
    New York
Whitney Miami (project), Miami, Florida

2003
Close Residence, Bridgehampton, New York
Dallas Museum of Art: Flora Court/East Entry, Dallas, Texas
Dumbacher Residence, New York, New York
GARDE/Untitled Shops Boutiques (project), Tokyo, Japan
High Line Competition (proposal), New York, New York
Jenny Holzer Porscheplatz Installation (project), Stuttgart, Germany
Helmut Lang Via Della Spiga, Milan, Italy
Helmut Lang Rue St. Honoré, Paris, France
Limpe Residence, New York, New York
Merrin Residence, New York, New York
Mori Arts Center, Tokyo, Japan
Tribeca Loft, New York, New York

2004
Benton Residence, East Hampton, New York
Dallas Museum of Art: Contemporary Galleries, Dallas, Texas
Edward Hopper Exhibition, Tate Modern, London, England
Lawler Residence, Brooklyn, New York
Lowry Residence, New York, New York
Meatpacking District/High Line Hotel (proposal), New York, New York
MoMA Design and Book Stores, New York, New York
Museo Picasso Malaga, Malaga, Spain
Revlon Showroom and Cafeteria, New York, New York
Rosen Residence, New York, New York
Sculpture Garden Pavilion, Bridgehampton, New York
Tony Shafrazi Gallery, New York, New York
Sotheby's 50 Rockefeller Center (project), New York, New York
Tsinghua University Art Museum (project), Beijing, China
University of Kentucky Art Museum (project), Lexington, Kentucky
Work in Process: Gluckman Mayner Designs the Perelman Building
    Exhibition, Philadelphia, Pennsylvania

2005
Dia: Beacon: Lower Level Galleries (project), Beacon, New York
Gluckman Mayner Architects: Making Frames Exhibition, Syracuse,
    New York
Goodman Residence (project), Cortez Island, British Columbia, Canada
Green Residence, Austin, Texas
Guggenheim Hermitage (project), St. Petersburg, Russia
Gummer Studio, Long Island City, New York
Hall Residence (project), New York, New York
Jenny Holzer Obelisk Installation, Berlin, Germany
Hotel Puerta America, Madrid, Spain
Iglesia Evangelica de Co-op City, Bronx, New York
Kelly Shear Studio and Archives, Columbia County, New York
Kouri Residence II, New York, New York
Parrish Art Museum (project), Southampton, New York
Philadelphia Antiques Show Exhibition, Philadelphia, Pennsylvania
Robin Hood Library for P.S. 192, New York, New York

St. Louis Art Museum (proposal), St. Louis, Missouri
Watermill Center, Watermill, New York
Wright Residence (project), Seattle, Washington

2006
Artist's Residence & Studio, Orient, New York
Central Park South Residence, New York, New York
Clemente Studio, Brooklyn, New York
Gagosian Gallery Twenty-first Street, New York, New York
The Guggenheim: Architecture Exhibition, Bonn, Germany
Guggenheim Foundation Offices, New York, New York
Guggenheim West Side (project), New York, New York
Kenyon Hall, Vassar College, Poughkeepsie, New York
Yvon Lambert Gallery, New York, New York
Marlborough Gallery at Chelsea Arts Tower, New York, New York
One Kenmare Square, New York, New York
200 Eleventh Avenue Tower (proposal), New York, New York
The Warehouse, Syracuse University, Syracuse, New York

2007
Albright-Knox Art Gallery (project), Buffalo, New York
Baum Residence, New York, New York
Faggionato Fine Arts (project), London, England
INV Building, Englewood Cliffs, New Jersey
Lowertown Development (project), St. Paul, Minnesota
MoMA Design Store, Tokyo, Japan
Museum of Contemporary Art San Diego, San Diego, California
Oeri/Bodenmann Residence II, New York, New York
Perelman Building, Philadelphia Museum of Art, Philadelphia,
    Pennsylvania
Robin Hood Libraries for P.S. 48X, P.S. 64X, P.S. 154X, P.S. 146M,
    and P.S. 189M, Bronx, New York, and New York, New York
Tenth Avenue Hotel (proposal), New York, New York
Weil/Camp Residence (project), Orient, New York

2008
Brant Foundation Art Study Center, Greenwich, Connecticut
Contemporary Architectural Drawings Exhibition, National Academy
    Museum, New York, New York
Contemporary Art Museum of the Presidio (project), San Francisco,
    California
Dallas Museum of Art: Center for Creative Connections/Horchow
    Auditorium, Dallas, Texas
Ervin Residence, Amagansett, New York
FLAG Art Foundation, New York, New York
Fundacio Sorigue (project), Lleida, Spain
GCAM Offices (project), New York, New York
Museum of Arts and Design Restaurant (project), New York, New York
Pace Beijing, Beijing, China
Qibao Culture Park (proposal), Shanghai, China

2009
Olive 8, Seattle, Washington
Cordy Ryman Residence, New York, New York

IN PROGRESS
Brand Residence, New York, New York
Cooper-Hewitt Expansion, New York, New York
Georgia Museum of Art, Athens, Georgia
Calvin Klein Studio, New York, New York
Lange Residence, Orient, New York
Mii amo Spa and Resort, Punta Mita, Mexico
Mii amo Villas, Sedona, Arizona
Milgrom Residence, Melbourne, Australia
Mott Residence, Sonoma, California
Perelman Residence, Grand Island, Bahamas
Saadiyat Temporary Cultural Park, Abu Dhabi, United Arab Emirates
Staten Island Museum at Snug Harbor, Staten Island, New York
Strüngmann Residence, Bridgehampton, New York
Syracuse University College of Law, Syracuse, New York
Zhejiang University Museum of Art and Archaeology, Hangzhou, China

PHOTOGRAPHY CREDITS

Numbers refer to page numbers. Drawings, renderings, and model photos (except where noted otherwise) © Gluckman Mayner Architects. Parenthetical notes identify main artworks and installations included in photographs.

© David S. Allee: 192 top, 193 bottom (left to right: Aristide Maillol sculpture, courtesy Ruth and Raymond Perelman; **Goddess Figure (Chalchiuhtlicue)**, made in central Mexico c. 250–65; Jacques Lipchitz, **The Prayer**, 1943; Joan Miró, **Lunar Bird**, 1966; Henry Moore, **Two Forms**, 1936)

© Amy Barkow: 152–58 (152–53: left: Yayoi Kusama, **Inward Vision No. 4**; right: Thomas Struth, **Pergamon Museum VI**; 154: Richard Hamilton, **Bathroom Figure 1**; 155 top: left: Hannah Hoch, **Streit (Quarrel)**; on coffee table: Tunga, **An Eye for an Eye**; right: Katharina Fritsch, **Hund (Dog)**; 155 bottom: left: Reneke Dijkstra, **Kolobrzeg, Poland, July 27, 1992**; center: Jeff Wall, **Diagonal Composition No. 3**; right: Richard Prince, **Untitled (the same man looking in different directions)**; 158 top and bottom left: Steve Wolfe, **Untitled (Joni Mitchell Help Me)**; 158 bottom right: Jeff Wall, **Diagonal Composition No. 3**, all courtesy of the owners)

© Bleda y Rosa: 77 top

© Eric Boman: 46–52 (48 bottom left: Richard Serra; 51 top: Mary Heilmann)

© Jimmy Cohrssen: 64 top, 64 bottom right, 65 top right, 65 bottom

© Lydia Gould Bessler: 24 bottom (installation: **David Salle, Pastoral,** © David Salle /VAGA, New York/DACS, London), 25 bottom (installation: Damien Hirst, © Damien Hirst/DACS), 28–31 (installation: Leonardo Drew; 30–31 background: Barbara Kruger), 32, 98–104 (103 top right: Antonio Murado; 103 bottom left: Richard Wright), 110–16

© John Hall: 12–13

© David Heald: 8–9, 10–11 (installation: **Cast a Cold Eye, The Late Works of Andy Warhol;** © Andy Warhol Foundation for the Visual Arts/ARS, New York), 74–76, 77 bottom, 78 top (Museo Picasso Malaga Permanent Collection, Gallery 8), 79, 80 (Temporary Exhibition Galleries, installation: **El Picasso de los Picasso**), 81–84, 122–23, 124 top (left: Ellsworth Kelly, **Diagonal with Curve X**, 1979; right: Ellsworth Kelly, **Untitled**, 1978), 124 top (far left: Ellsworth Kelly, **Untitled**, 2004), 124 bottom (left: Ellsworth Kelly, **Diagonal with Curve XIII**, 1980; right: Ellsworth Kelly, **White Diagonal**, 2007), 125 top (left: Ellsworth Kelly, **Black Diagonal II**, 2008; center: Ellsworth Kelly, **Blue Diagonal**, 2008; right: Ellsworth Kelly, **White Diagonal**, 2007), 125 bottom, 126, 128–33, 134 (Mark Raush), 164–68 (installation: **Cast a Cold Eye, The Late Works of Andy Warhol;** © Andy Warhol Foundation for the Visual Arts/ARS, New York), 170–78 (172–73, 176, 177 top: Jenny Holzer, **For MCASD**, 2007; 175 top:

Ernesto Neto, **Mother body emotional densities,/for alive temple time baby son**, 2007; 174 bottom, 178: Richard Serra, **Santa Fe Depot**, 2007), 190–91, 192 bottom, 193 top (John Chamberlain, **Glossalia Adagio**, 1984), 194, 195 (left to right: John Chamberlain, **Glossalia Adagio**, 1984; Jacques Lipchitz, **The Prayer**, 1943; Toshiko Takaezu, **Li-Mu (Seaweed)**, 1993), 196 top, 196 bottom (Paul Manship, **The Four Elements: Earth, Wind, Fire, and Water**, 1914), 197 top (installation: **A Conversation in Three Dimensions: Sculpture from the Collections:** foreground left: Richard Long, **Limestone Circle**, 1985; right: Martin Puryear, **Generation**, 1988; in background, left to right: Phoebe Adams, **All Most**, 1989; Sol LeWitt, **Splotch**, 2003; Anselm Kiefer, **Palette with Wings**, 1985; Jean Dubuffet, **Landscape with Tree**, 1968–69), 197 bottom, 198 (left to right: Henry Moore, **Two Forms**, 1936; **Goddess Figure (Chalchiuhtlicue)**, made in central Mexico c. 250–65; Jacques Lipchitz, **The Prayer**, 1943; Toshiko Takaezu, **Li-Mu (Seaweed)**, 1993), 200–204

© Nikolas Koenig: 86–90 (Isamu Noguchi; Donald Judd), 144–46, 148–50

© Kudo Photo: 62–63, 64 bottom left

© Thomas Loof and Pernille Pedersen: 92–96

© Peter Mauss/Esto: 106–8

© Robert McKeever, courtesy Gagosian Gallery: 25 top (Richard Serra, **No Relief**, 2006)

© Frank Oudeman: 147

© Jock Pottle: 34–37, 54–56, 162

© Tim Street-Porter: 136–42

© Hiroshi Sugimoto: 66 (installation: **Hiroshi Sugimoto, End of Time**, courtesy Hiroshi Sugimoto)

© Hiroshi Ueda: cover, 6–7, 58–61, 65 top left

© Yasuhito Yagi: 184–88

© Harry Zernike: 20–21(installation: **Richard Serra: Torqued Spirals, Toruses and Spheres:** left: **Bellamy**, 2001; right: **Sylvester**, 2001), 22–23 (Richard Serra, **Betwixt the Torus and the Sphere**, 2001), 24 top, 26 (left: Richard Serra, **Sylvester**, 2001; right: Richard Serra, **Bellamy**, 2001), 38–44, 68–69 (left: Ellsworth Kelly, **Red Green Blue**, 2002; on table: Greg Lynn FORM, **Tea and Coffee Tower**, 2003; on floor: Robert Gober, **Untitled (Two Elements)**, 2000–2001, all courtesy of the owners), 70–71 (70 top left, 70 bottom right, 71 bottom left: Brice Marden, **Black Frieze**, 1987; 70 top foreground, 70 bottom left: Katharina Fritsch, **Warengestell II (Display Stand II)**, 2001; 70 top on floor: Robert Gober, **Untitled (Two Elements)**, 2000–2001; 70 top right: Gerhard Richter, **Abstraktes Bild, Dunkel**, 1986; 70 bottom center: Thomas Ruff, **Substrat 11 II**, 2003; 71 top: Andreas Gursky, **Rhein II**, 1999; 71 bottom center: Jean-Marc Bustamante, **T.7.01**, 2001; 71 bottom right: Richard Hamilton, **Ghosts of Ufa**, 1995, all courtesy of the owners), 72